HOW TO READ

Palms

HOW TO READ
Palms

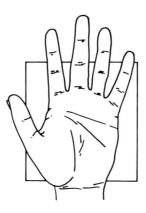

HAMLYN

This edition published in 1989 by
The Hamlyn Publishing Group Limited,
a division of the Octopus Publishing Group,
Michelin House,
81 Fulham Road,
London SW3 6RB

Text and illustrations taken from the work
Conoscerti, Enciclopedia dei Test
© 1986 Gruppo Editoriale Fabbri SpA
Milan

©1988 Octopus Books Limited

ISBN 0 600 56776 1

Produced by Mandarin Offset.
Printed and bound in Hong Kong.

Contents

Introduction

Is there a precise relationship between the structure of the hand and the character? This question has long aroused intense interest and it is remarkable that palmists in different countries have come independently to the same conclusions about the significance of the lines, shape and colour of the hand. In the seventeenth century, palmistry became a university subject and was most commonly taught in Germany, before it dwindled slightly in popularity. However, scholars did not allow that wealth of accumulated knowledge to be lost, and the names of great palmists are still famous today, including that of Casimir Stanislas d'Arpentigny, one of the fathers of modern palmistry. He classified the hand shapes into the types that are still referred to today: spatulate, square, elementary, conic, psychic, philosophic and mixed.

Palmistry is a science and does not call for any psychic powers on the part of the practitioner. A relaxed consultation and an atmosphere of trust between you and your subject is what you should be looking for; in such a situation your subject will use his or her hands, those most expressive parts of the body, in a natural fashion and you will be able to deduce a good deal about character just from his or her gestures. As your experience grows, so you will be able to pick up the tiny nuances which help to build a complete picture.

With images of fairground fortune-tellers in mind, some people think that palmistry consists simply of reading the lines of the palm. This is not so. The shape of the hand, its colour, temperature and texture, the form and arrangement of the fingers, the shape of the nails, must all be taken into account. You should never make a judgement based on the lines of the palm without considering the other features of the hand, to see if they confirm or deny your finding. It was the fortune-teller's practice of drawing conclusions from the palmar lines alone that gave palmistry a bad reputation, from which it has only recovered in the past 50 years. During this time it has become accepted as a reliable means of assessing character: take a responsible approach and you will not join the long list of dubious practitioners!

It is also recognized that the signs of some illnesses can be detected in the hand long before and after their symptoms are manifested in the rest of the body. Psychiatrists may study the hand in order to obtain information about the nature of a mental illness they are attempting to treat, or the progress of an organic disease may be monitored by repeated hand readings. In this way, palmistry has become accepted by the medical profession as a useful tool in some diagnoses.

This book takes a comprehensive look at the science of hand analysis. The first chapter looks at the shape of the hand, its temperature, type and skin colour, and explains the meaning of such terms as the 'psychic hand' and the 'philosophic hand'. Having mastered the significance of the whole hand in Chapter 1, Chapter 2 describes to you the meaning held by the lines of head, heart, life, Apollo (sun), Mercury (temperament) and Saturn (fate). In Chapter 3, the minor lines and marks, including those of travel, marriage and children, are examined and the technique of taking a palm print explained.

The mounts of Venus, Jupiter, Saturn, Apollo, Mercury, Mars and the Moon have a telling role in hand analysis and the fourth chapter takes each mount and explains the part it plays. Chapter 5 analyses the shape of the fingers and the significance of their alignment to each other, while also explaining the relationship between the phalanges (lengths of bone) of each finger.

Next comes an enlightening chapter on a fascinating branch of palmistry, established by the ancient civilization of China many thousands of years ago. The Chinese look at the patterns made by some of the line intersections in the palm, and interpret them symbolically. Finally, a 'Questions and Answers' chapter deals with some common queries that arise about certain features of the hand. You should now be well equipped to embark on reading your first palm – a first step on a voyage of discovery into this uniquely illuminating method of understanding the hidden features of the human character. The science of palmistry has been held in deep regard by scholars over thousands of years. Hippocrates and Aristotle knew of and respected it; it is referred to more than once in the Bible. In our own times, modern psychology places great importance on the appearance of the hand as an indication of the physical wellbeing and mental make-up of its owner. So what is this ancient lore and how can you learn it?

As with all branches of knowledge, the more you study the more you know. A true appreciation of the significance of the hand takes much learning and considerable experience in studying different hands. However, many of the lines and formations are quite easy to recognize and it is not long before the beginner can draw a considerable amount of information from a proffered palm. As you progress, you will start to pick out the fainter and more elusive portents of your subject's character and – who knows? – you may soon stumble across some of the more uncommon signs that appear in very few hands. One thing is certain – once you have begun your study of palmistry you will never be able to resist glancing at a stranger's hand!

1

The Hand

The basic shape and type of the hand holds a wealth of information as to the character of its owner. When doing a hand analysis, never draw conclusions from the palmar lines without also taking into account whether the hand is small, large, broad, narrow, short or long; whether it can be classified as elementary, useful, active, philosophic, artistic, psychic or mixed. Consider the colour, too – is it pink, white, yellow or reddish? Is the hand cold, hot, damp or dry? You may well find blemishes that betray physiological problems as well as psychological characteristics.

The hand may appear a very different shape when viewed from the back rather than from the front and in palmistry the shape is always determined from the palmar side. As to the temperature, bear in mind that if you have seated your subject in front of a fire or next to an open window on a chilly day you may be exerting considerable influence over your findings. Likewise, be aware that if you have not created a sufficiently relaxed atmosphere the damp hands of your unfortunate subject may simply be due to nervous tension, and you should not jump to any immediate conclusions.

The signs in a hand

Shape

The shape of the hand reveals much about character. The hand may be large or small in relation to the body, wide or narrow in relation to the wrist, fat or thin, hard or soft. It will give you an immediate general idea of a person's character.

The large hand

This belongs to egocentric and thoughtful individuals who analyse all questions in depth before taking a decision, but do not then change their minds. It indicates constancy, pride and considerable physical and nervous strength. This is the hand of individuals in whom reason prevails over the heart.

The small hand

This is typical of sensitive and lively people who immediately take in situations and concepts. It reveals intuition, impulsiveness, a spirit of adaptability, a cheerful temperament, but also a certain tendency to be slapdash. Sometimes it also indicates a tendency to tell white lies.

The broad hand

This reveals a broad outlook, self-confidence, dynamism. The faults of this person are tactlessness, thoughtlessness and vanity; good qualities are optimism, benevolence and frankness with others.

The narrow hand

People with narrow hands tend to close in on themselves either from pride or fear. Very often, they exhibit physical weakness. In females, this type of hand may indicate periods of infertility (which are curable).

The short hand

These belong to disorganized, impatient and thoughtless people who allow themselves to be influenced by others and often act on impulse. They are capricious and loquacious.

The long hand

This reveals caution, thoughtfulness, commonsense and calculation. Decisions are taken slowly and with circumspection. It indicates an ability to get around obstacles.

The hard hand

This is an indication of practicality, considerable vigour and passion and a need for action. It is common in determined and courageous people with a strong grasp of reality, who show scant imagination and a degree of intransigence.

The soft hand

These belong to the apathetic dreamers who detest physical effort. It denotes laziness and a lack of will-power but it also signifies an incredible astuteness whereby the owner is able to draw material and moral advantage from every situation. It belongs to people who live independently, doing only what they want to do and getting away with it!

The chubby hand

This is very similar in terms of its meaning to the large hand. It indicates constancy, energy, an enjoyment of good food, a desire for material possessions and a highly erotic imagination. It belongs to people who dislike being alone.

The thin hand

This indicates an introverted, melancholy nature, a lack of vitality and a tendency to give up easily. It does, however, show a vivid imagination and an ability to experience strong emotions and spiritual joy.

The hot hand

This indicates a communicative person who openly expresses what he or she is feeling, and participates in the joys and sorrows of others. It also indicates a love of drama, a tendency to exaggerate and a quick temper.

The cold hand

This belongs to a person who knows how to hide his or her feelings either out of shyness or for personal gain. It denotes a state of anxiety and possibly conceals hidden passion.

The damp hand

This is a distinctive feature of lazy, sensual individuals who may be of low moral fibre. If the dampness is temporary, it indicates only shyness and emotion. From a clinical point of view, a damp hand is regarded as being closely connected to the lymphatic system: it reveals lymphatic and digestive problems.

The dry hand

This belongs to a person who suppresses his or her feelings in order for reason to prevail. It denotes a closed character.

Colour

The colour of the hand not only provides information as to the owner's character, it also indicates health problems.

The pink hand

A balanced, sane person capable of self-control is revealed in this hand.

The white hand

This shows an apathetic and materialistic temperament that seeks wellbeing and physical gratification. It indicates a desire to receive love, but an unwillingness to give it.

The yellow hand

This denotes an irritable and nervous temperament that continually seeks new experiences. It indicates intuition and individualism and, in some cases, fanaticism.

The ruddy hand
This hand is found in cheerful, passionate individuals who let themselves be led solely by instinct, sometimes resulting in excess. It is associated with courage, anger, inconstancy and frankness.

The darkly coloured hand
This denotes a controlled and severe character with strong, slow reactions. There is a possibility of biliary disorders.

Blemishes
Like the colour of the hand, blemishes are a valuable guide to the state of health of the owner.

Blue blemishes
These indicate shyness, irritability and melancholia. If the blemishes are under the thumb, they indicate sexual weakness; if elsewhere, the risk of intoxication of the intestines or liver.

Red blemishes
These are associated with disturbances of the circulation. A ruddy fingertip around the nail is a sign of nervousness and sensuality.

Yellow blemishes
These can be a sign of a liver or kidney disorder. If the yellow is dark or brownish, especially under the ring finger, it can indicate eye problems.

Dark or almost black blemishes
These denote poor functioning of the bile and liver. Dark blemishes may be a precursor of typhoid fever.

Left
Margaret Thatcher's hand is large and pale. A large hand is indicative of determination to see through decisions and belongs to those for whom reason prevails over the emotions. A pale hand shows a certain amount of discipline and self-control

Right
Beethoven's chubby hands signal great imaginative powers

Types of hand

In the past, scholars managed to classify over a hundred different types of hand. However, relatively recent studies by great experts such as Desbarolles and D'Arpentigny have established that there are seven basic types of hand, connected with the same number of human temperaments. The classification is based on the proportion between the fingers and the palm, and on the overall profile.

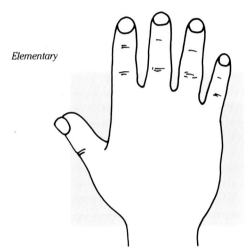

Elementary

The elementary hand

This is the most common and simple type of hand. It is rather large and chubby, with a hard palm and short stubby fingers. The thumb is turned back, often reaching as far as the base of the index finger. In general, on examining the palm, few clear lines with specific characteristics will be seen.

Character

Normally, this hand belongs to people who perform manual work and who have scant intellectual interests. This does not mean that they lack intelligence. They have simply yielded to routine and refuse to devote their minds to any thought that requires strength of will. They are prepared to put up with physical fatigue without complaining and they have a kind of fatalistic resignation.

People with an elementary hand love everything relating to nature – plants, flowers, animals. They have a strong maternal or paternal instinct, and enjoy being in the company of children. They are patient, but beware of annoying them! They can exhibit an excess of anger, for however short a time. These individuals rarely fall prey to nervous disorders; they do, however, need to beware of organic disorders.

The useful hand

This hand is almost square-shaped, both in the palm and in the fingers. The thumb is large, wide and well developed at the base. The middle finger is shorter than normal and the joints tend to be well-developed. The nails look stumpy and, again, square.

Character

This is the typical hand of someone who knows how to organize himself or herself, who is pragmatic, and has a firmly based view of reality. For this individual, the only thing that counts is logic, and he or she will have difficulty in tolerating abstract discussions of metaphysics. Such people want to get straight to the point, to the tangible. Their behaviour is honest, precise, ordered; in any discussion, they will refer back to the law and to morals. Their relationships with others are not always easy, as they tend to annoy them with their fastidiousness. However, they are ultimately respected for their upright character.

Through their qualities of patience and perseverance, they frequently attain sought-after goals. The most likely professions for these individuals are in law, medicine, marketing, teaching, architecture, accountancy and economics. They are usually very closely tied to their family, faithful to their partner and good at bringing up their children (albeit a little rigidly).

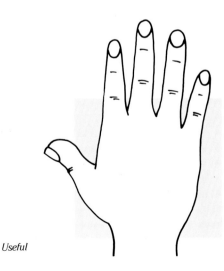

Useful

The picture of Marco Polo shows him with a typically active hand – long fingers, spatulate fingertips and a high, flattened thumb

The active hand

This hand is irregular in structure: the fingers are a little longer than the hand, the fleshy parts of the fingertips are spatulate, the thumb high and flattened, the nails long and flat.

Character

It is known as the active hand because it belongs to individuals with a dynamic, enterprising temperament – individuals who never allow themselves a moment's rest and who, in their untiring quest for novelty and experience, create a tumultuous life for themselves. Their character is optimistic, exuberant and inquisitive about everything. They move in a wide range of circles and activities, showing considerable versatility. In love they are often irresistible and overwhelming, but they need a partner who knows how to follow them in their numerous enthusiasms. The professions in which they succeed best are those that require a spirit of adventure and physical energy: they are explorers, travellers, sailors, runners or sportsmen. However, they are also capable of asserting themselves in the field of science and engineering. They have frequent highs and lows in their careers, but they know how to pick themselves up and start again.

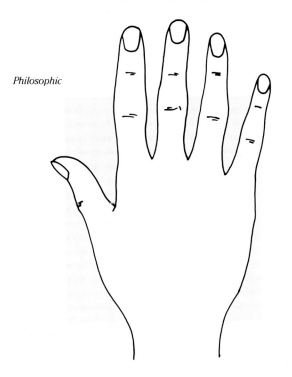

Philosophic

The philosophic hand

This is also known as the 'knotty hand', as the fingers are exaggeratedly bony and elastic. The palm is usually broad, the thumb large and pointed, the fleshy tips of the fingers tapered and thin, and the nails long.

Character

This hand belongs to people who are interested in intellectual and cultural pursuits. It is the hand of the thinker, philosopher and moralist. For them, what is important is not social and material success but adherence to their own principles. They have a strong and attractive personality and know how to fascinate others with their profound ideas. In their actions they do not allow themselves to be influenced by contrary opinions, being firm in their decisions.

They surround themselves with a limited number of friends of a certain mental level, but they also like extroverted and extravagant individuals, provided they are talented. In spite of their precise moral and religious convictions, they are broadminded in their judgment of others. They are attracted by the mystery of life and death, of everything that is intangible and transcendental. In romantic relationships they are loyal and faithful, although they tend to idealize their partners and fail to take account of their specific requirements. Hopeless at practical activities, they are likely to gain esteem as philosophers, teachers, writers or members of the clergy.

The artistic hand

Of average, conical dimensions, well-proportioned, with long, smooth and possibly pointed fingers, the artistic hand is generally soft and light.

Character

This is the typical artist's hand (in the aesthetic/romantic, as well as the literal, sense). It denotes a sensitive, inconstant, dreaming, impulsive and emotive nature which looks for sensations, atmospheres and unusual experiences.

People with this hand follow the extravagances of fashion and are attracted by the most reckless situations without heeding the consequences. They fall in love easily, living their relationships in an intense and chaotic fashion: moments of great passion alternate with sudden coldness. Always ready to act on behalf of friendship and sentiment, they do not want to assume serious responsibility.

They are always outgoing, but anyone who spends time with them continuously will discover their weaknesses and secret fears. They are not lovers of everyday domestic life, and if forced to live such an existence will escape it through their fantasies.

The owners of this hand may be found in the artistic or design fields, in the antique business or in any activity that also requires an aesthetic sense.

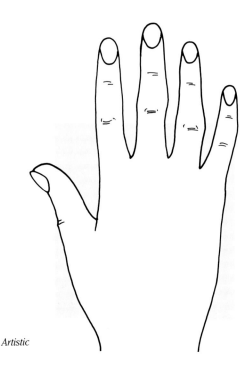

Artistic

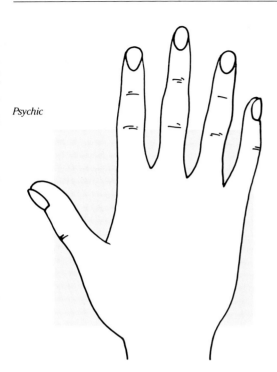

Psychic

The mixed hand

This hand does not fit into any precise type, but is a combination of various aspects of the other six types of hand. It is extremely widespread, since most people have a personality which is somewhat contradictory and complex.

Character

The owners of a mixed hand do not exhibit any marked tendencies. They are adaptable to every circumstance and have a marked practical sense enabling them to carry out tasks at home and at work with ease. They are versatile and lively with a wide circle of friends, and enjoy a reasonably active social life, being neither extreme introverts nor extroverts.

If they have a problem they confront it squarely, so that ultimately they are able to surmount obstacles with ease and the daily pattern of their lives remains unaffected.

If they have a monotonous life, they know how to liven it up with various hobbies and interests, as those with a mixed hand are resourceful and motivated. Emotionally strong but not impervious, sometimes inner conflict can cause them psychosomatic disorders, but these individuals are able to restore their own equilibrium within a short period of time. Altogether theirs is a naturally balanced constitution and they take life as it comes.

The psychic hand

Aesthetically this is the most beautiful, harmonious and elegant hand; it has a narrow, oval palm, long, smooth fingers without pronounced joints and long, almond-shaped nails. It should not be confused with the artistic hand which is long but not necessarily elegant and smooth. This hand is rarely found in the West, but is widespread in India and in the Far East.

Character

This is the hand of a person who has a contemplative, imaginative character and tends to live detached from reality, taking refuge in the world of dreams and ideals. Such people find their spiritual fulfilment in the quest for all things poetic and exalted.

The owners of a psychic hand will be taciturn with people who do not understand them, and loquacious with those who are in accord. They have formidable intuition at psychic level, often embrace oriental religions and are interested in the occult. They detest day-to-day pettiness, the struggle for money and for success and rate mysticism and ideals above them. They experience wonderful, but unrealistic, love affairs but are easily hurt both because they are too trusting and because their feelings are very near the surface. Unfortunately these people rarely seem to learn by their mistakes and are best off living a contemplative life in remote, scenic places where society exercises few demands on them.

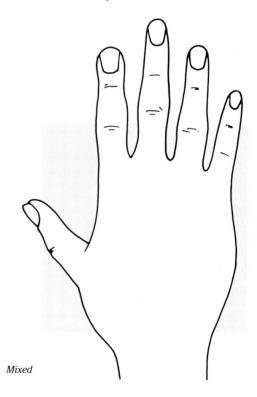

Mixed

2

Major Lines

The major lines are the most well-known aspect of palmistry – who has not heard of the life line or the heart line? Many people claim to be able to read them but in reality the significance of these lines can be altered by a number of tiny details – for example, a branch may mean all the difference between a confident, cheerful person and a timid, depressive one.

The lines of heart, life and fate hold the most fascination for the majority of people. Certainly, to discover that one is the owner of a heart line that ends on the Mount of Saturn, auguring the greatest happiness in love, life and work, would lift the clouds on even the gloomiest day. On the other hand, you may find yourself in a position to reassure the apprehensive owner of a short or broken life line that this is not an omen of impending death.

As always in palmistry, you must not jump to conclusions on the strength of one line. If it is not repeated on the other hand it bears little significance and, of course, you must seek further evidence in the shape and type of the whole hand and the fingers.

The life line

A long, well-defined life line describing a broad curve, also present in the right hand, indicates physical exuberance and mental acuity. The nervous system is in perfect balance, and provides both physical and intellectual strength with considerable resistance to stress.

Owners of this type of life line are always ready to give their best because they are aware of the difficulties of life and the demands that will be made on them. It typically belongs to the hands of those who have attained a position of considerable importance and who are endowed with the necessary amount of drive to maintain it.

A well-defined life line also indicates the happy facility of finding the right solution to any problem. This suggests a noble quality: a deep bond with nature, accompanied by the instinctive ability to understand the significance of the events in which the individual is involved.

A coarse or red life line, however, is characteristic of those who have both a robust constitution and a possibly irascible nature. The latter may lead them to fall victim to their own impulsiveness and hasty temper. This fault is, however, mitigated by sincerity and a sense of justice.

A weak physique and complicated personality are revealed by a pallid, broad life line. Characteristic features that may be associated with this type of life line are feelings of envy and an indifference to the complexities of life.

A life line that is more marked at the beginning (at the mount of Venus) expresses a passionate and, at the same time, receptive, nature; if, however, it is more marked at the end, it means that the individual tends to assert himself or herself in all circumstances, with the result that he or she appears somewhat argumentative.

A broken and irregular life line indicates a timid individual: a wavy line, on the other hand, denotes a strong character but one which is subject to isolated bursts of anger.

Interruptions in the line of life indicate that good care of the health is needed. The owner of a line that starts at the base of the thumb will be very hardheaded, a person who is more prone to analysis than to any artistic talent; the true leader will have a life line which is on both hands connected either to the line of the head or to the line of the heart. A sense of control and the right amount of aggression, decision and charisma are this individual's best qualities.

If the life line ends with short parallel lines it denotes a nervous individual who suffers from unspecified fears.

Branches

A line that opens out into two obvious branches belongs in most cases to a fortunate person for whom the future holds long journeys, exciting changes, and a whole series of satisfying experiences.

If the life line shows a branch in the direction of the Mount of Jupiter, intelligent use of the owner's personal qualities will lead to success.

A branch in the life line towards the Mount of the Moon is a passport to the world of fantasy, inspiration and romanticism.

When the branch points in the direction of the head line, the owner must take care not to become easily discouraged; difficulties in life can be overcome with will power.

If the life line bends towards the heart line, this indicates that the owner is easily swayed and should put greater reliance on his or her own abilities.

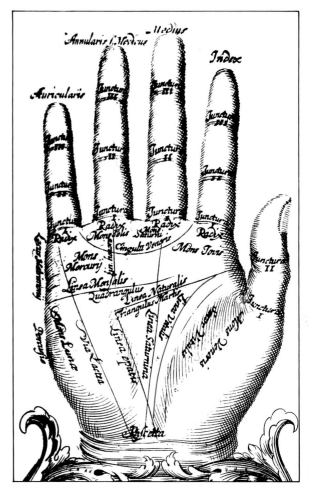

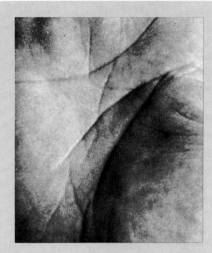

Left
This is a lucky person's long and well-defined life line, which ends with two branches

Right
This deep, pronounced life line shows irascibility but also a sense of justice

Left
This life line exhibits a series of interruptions and branches, each of which is significant

Right
An interrupted life line away from the head line, showing marked rationality

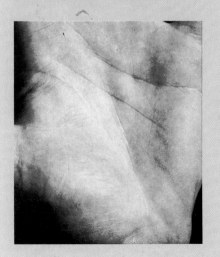

Left
A thin but very clear life line, indicating shyness, sensitivity and reflectiveness

Right
The striking confusion of branches in this life line belongs to an apprehensive person

The head line

The head line reveals intellectual capacity and potential. It has a number of different starting points – the Mount of Jupiter, the life line, inside the life line – and travels towards the percussion (side of the hand). The meanings of its various positions are outlined here. An important feature of the head line is that when it curves towards the Mount of Mars or the Mount of the Moon the characteristics of the line will be reinforced.

If the head line is long and well formed both in the right hand and in the left, the intellect and social conscience will be very well developed. This fortunate person also possesses a warm nature, adding a touch of passion to their sense of justice and idealism. A good memory is a further bonus.

A deep, red head line denotes a proud but easily influenced character, possibly liable to magnify his or her fears. If the line is pale and broad, the owner's suggestibility is even more exaggerated.

Anyone who has a head line that intersects the entire palm of the hand is destined to enjoy considerable material success. He or she will have an eclectic mind with the logical precision of a Swiss watch! Their only fault will be a tendency towards greed.

If the head line is frequently interrupted, this is an indication of the owner's desire for self improvement, of good will, but also of inconstancy.

A wavy head line indicates imagination and creative ability – but beware, there is a risk of magnifying problems for no reason.

A line that starts in a fork indicates an optimistic temperament, rich in ideas; this person will find it very easy to gain other people's confidence. However, a line that ends in a fork is found in lively, decisive people with just the right amount of practicality.

If the hand contains a head line that starts from the Mount of Jupiter, its owner will undoubtedly be vain; but if the line also touches the life line, their characteristic features will be intelligence and a sense of proportion.

A person who has a head line that starts from the level of Mars will be irritable, talkative and rather egotistic.

If the head line extends as far as the Mount of the Moon it belongs to an imaginative, artistic person. However, someone who has a line extending to the Mount of Mercury will have an innate business ability, although professional success is usually associated with a branch towards the Mount of Apollo.

A branch towards the heart line is found in people who are governed by their feelings, given to depression and who live in a dream world. However, a branch that reaches the outer edge of the palm is said to belong to those who achieve widespread fame – or at least notoriety – for their life's work.

Sometimes a double head line appears on one hand, usually on the right hand. It indicates that this person lives a dual life. Often it belongs to someone who has two entirely different careers – he or she might be self-employed and have a full time position with an employer. Very often these people keep their two lifestyles or careers separate, so that few people who know them in one capacity know of the other.

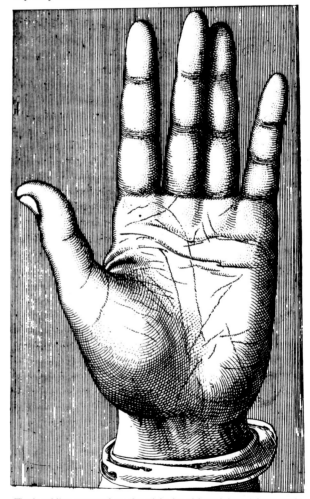

The head line crosses the palm of the hand from left to right towards the Mount of Mars or the Mount of the Moon. This line provides information about the strength of the intellect and about the state of the nervous system. More than any other line, this line will tell you how the individual reacts to external stimuli

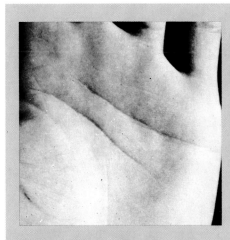

Left
This head line starts in a fork, indicating naturalness with others and a lively mind

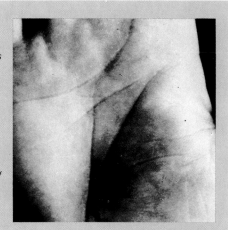

Right
The head line ends at the Plain of Mars, revealing a strong-willed, calculating person

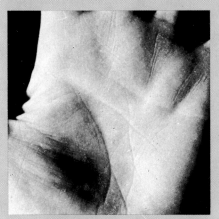

Left
When the head line extends to the Mount of Mars, as here, instinct prevails over reason

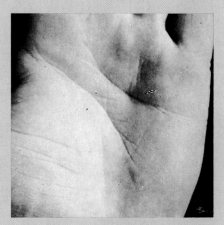

Right
If the head line ends with a fork, decisiveness and a spirit of initiative are indicated

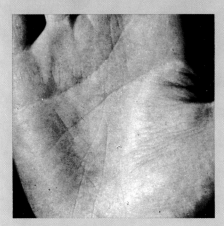

Left
The thin head line illustrated shows a generous, but sometimes capricious, person

Right
Here the two branches towards the Mount of Mars and the Mount of the Moon show creativity

The heart line

The heart line contains the key to the finer feelings of which the human soul is capable. Its origin is located between the Mount of Mercury and the Mount of Mars, symbolizing the eternal battle between the forces of intellect and instinct. The individual aspects of the heart line indicate which force tends to prevail.

If the line is long and well-defined in both the right and the left hands, this denotes a good and fair nature. Generosity, involvement in the problems of others and kindness are always to be found in these individuals. In addition, they are unselfish, capable of true friendship and have an inner serenity.

The situation changes when the hand shows a coarse, red heart line. In this case, sensual love and attraction to the opposite sex will prevail. These urges are, however, mitigated by a sense of duty, and by an ability to keep promises.

A pale, wide heart line indicates a tendency towards sentimentality. However, this is balanced by a tranquil nature.

People who have a heart line that is more marked at the beginning are extremely cheerful. Others find them likeable, since they are outgoing, expansive and lively. More or less the same applies to individuals who have a marked line at the end: they are strong, practical and impulsive – although the latter quality is kept under control.

The wavy or chained heart line reveals a love of occasional adventures and of brief flirtations. If the line is broken, beware of binding relationships with the owner. This line indicates a tendency to start petty tiffs with one's partner and an extremely jealous nature.

People who have a heart line that is far away from both the head line and the life line are always satisfied with their lot, carefree and happy. This joie de vivre is also a frequent characteristic of the owners of a line that begins in a fork shape. They know how to give the best of themselves to friends and they throw their weight behind just causes; they are courteous, spontaneous and self-sacrificing.

A heart line that ends in a fork, however, is indicative of a dynamic, yet possibly egocentric, character.

A line with a number of branches is found in people who lack perseverance. Because of this their efforts are frequently met with disappointment and this can lead to depression and lack of confidence.

Maximum happiness awaits the owner of a heart line that ends on the Mount of Saturn. These people are truly blessed; they are happy in love, successful in business and in life, and have inner serenity. However, their good fortune is not mere luck as they are always level-headed individuals, able to capitalize on their advantages.

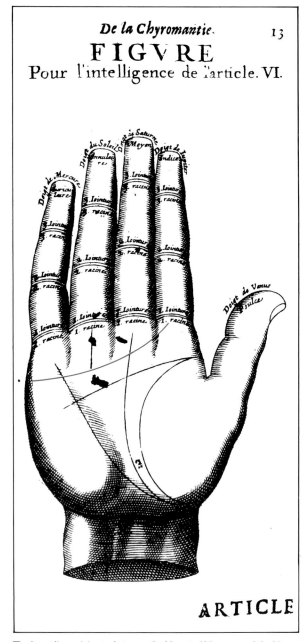

The heart line originates between the Mount of Mercury and the Mount of Mars and symbolizes the eternal conflict between reason and instinct, logic and passion. Other schools of thought see that this line ends on the Mount of Mercury or on the Mount of Mars, and begins on or near the Mount of Jupiter

Left
An interrupted heart line belongs to someone disturbed by inner worries and anxieties

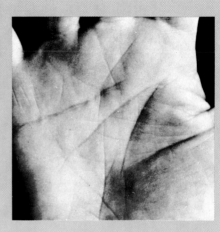

Right
When there are a number of branches from the heart line, the person is easily distracted

Left
A heart line beginning with a fork shows altruism, spontaneity and dedication

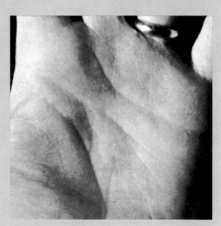

Right
The heart line runs towards the Mount of Jupiter revealing a commitment to loved ones

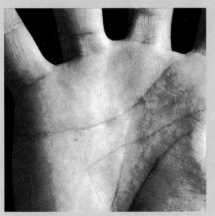

Left
A chained heart line ending on the Mount of Jupiter means adventures come before emotional ties

Right
A branch in the heart line leading towards the Mount of Jupiter shows a marriage crisis

The line of Apollo

The line of Apollo, or of success, is one of the secondary signs contained in the palm of the hand, but is no less important for that. It has a basically positive value: it is the line that presides over the harmonious development of events, and the happy solution to problems.

If the line of Apollo is long, well-defined and drawn along the axis from the base of the hand to the Mount of Apollo, its favourable influence will enhance the owner's life. People who have this type of line will achieve success and recognition: it indicates sensitivity, idealism and an artistic nature. Generosity and altruism will come to the rescue of the owners of such a line in moments of difficulty (which will be rare).

A line of Apollo that starts at the centre of the hand indicates that recognition will be gained, although sacrifices will have to be made to achieve it. The owner of this hand, therefore, must be prepared to wait for success that will eventually crown a career that is built up gradually.

When the line starts at the base of the hand, it indicates that spiritual matters are more important than material possessions. Creativity and high-mindedness are the distinguishing features in this person's day-to-day behaviour.

An Apollo line that starts from the life line reveals a balanced and highly principled character.

If the line starts from the Mount of the Moon, this means that people close to the subject will have a decisive role in his or her achievements.

A sharp intellect and a large amount of energy will create excellent opportunities for those who have an Apollo line that starts from the Mount of Mars. Their principal defect is a tendency towards egotism.

If the Apollo line is frequently interrupted along its length, this is a sign of a talented person who suffers from indecisiveness. Such people may never make the most of their capabilities.

A rather short line of Apollo indicates that the subjects will have to wait until the age of about 45 before reaching the peak of their profession. However, they will then occupy a position affording respect coupled with plenty of money.

Talkativeness, scattiness and inconstancy are the characteristics of people whose hand shows a wavy line of Apollo. Highs and lows are to be expected.

A line of Apollo flanked by a number of small parallel lines signifies broadmindedness, a wealth of interests and strong intuitive powers. If the upper part of the hand has a number of vertical lines, this means that the subject will experience alternating periods of optimism and depression. He or she will be more vulnerable, both physically and mentally, than average.

A double line of Apollo, accompanied by another pair of vertical lines, signifies a person of considerable intellect and business flair. He or she will always be ready to explore new avenues to extend his or her spheres of activity.

The Apollo line (line of the Sun) reveals aspects of the character liable to have the greatest influence on success at work. It has been regarded as an indication of happiness in life and of a bright future since palmistry's earliest days. It generally runs from near the wrist to the base of the Apollo finger and is sometimes mistaken for the line of Mercury as they both occupy similar positions

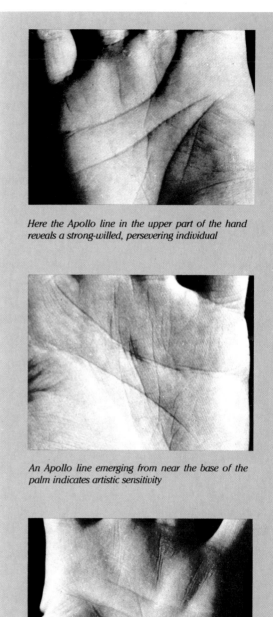

Here the Apollo line in the upper part of the hand reveals a strong-willed, persevering individual

An Apollo line emerging from near the base of the palm indicates artistic sensitivity

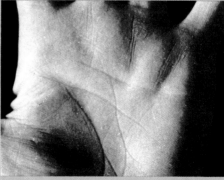

Small vertical lines replacing the Apollo line show a life punctuated by high and low points

The line of Mercury

The line of Mercury, or the Hepatica, occupies the space between the base of the hand and the Mount of Mercury. It is classified as one of the secondary signs although it is extremely important in evaluating mood changes and the balance of the nervous system. A line of Mercury with positive characteristics indicates an ability to cope serenely and successfully with the unexpected.

A long and well-defined line of Mercury has not always been interpreted in the same way. Usually it reveals strong nerves, intelligence, well-developed intuition and exceptional will power, often accompanied by a receptive nature and a good memory. The mind of a subject who has this wonderful line of Mercury will be ready to be stimulated, thanks to a natural flexibility. Other qualities that it indicates are generosity and kindliness in dealing with other people.

A long and very thin line of Mercury belongs to a somewhat talkative person who constantly seeks perfection. When the line is thin but widens towards the end, it indicates a studious subject with a calm disposition and enviable physical and mental health.

If the line is located in the upper part of the palm, this indicates problems in communicating with others and in coming to terms with events. However, these people have talent of a scientific and technical nature.

A line of Mercury in the lower part of the hand indicates introspection, far-sightedness and a reflective nature. When it is interrupted, it denotes a pronounced imagination and some degree of ambition.

A wavy line is a sign of eccentricity and shows a propensity for taking risks.

Nervous energy is indicated by a double line of Mercury, or one that is flanked by small vertical lines. Beware of overloading work on a nervous system that cannot cope with the strain.

A straight line of Mercury consisting of a number of vertical lines indicates periods of nervous exhaustion which will require rest to recover from.

It is a good sign to have a line that starts at the Mount of Venus, as this is generally a feature of people who are calm, serene and confident of their personal and professional abilities.

A line of Mercury that starts from the life line reveals that the owner will achieve fulfilment in life, as high principles and decisiveness are perfectly matched.

Branches

If the Mercury line shows a branch towards the Mount of Apollo, the subject's intellectual qualities will be well developed and continually enriched by further study.

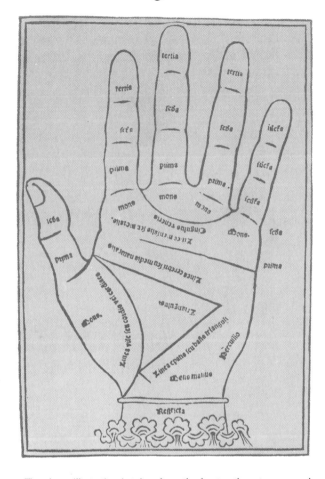

The above illustration is taken from the fourteenth-century manual Chiromantia, *by Achillinus-Coces of Milan. The manual describes all of the principal lines of the hand. The line of Mercury falls between the base of the hand and the Mount of Mercury and reveals a person's temperament and the balance of his or her nervous system. It can also indicate actual or imagined problems with health*

If the branch runs towards the Mount of Mars this is a symptom of a courageous nature capable of gaining respect from others and of a strong will to achieve prestigious goals.

A branch towards the Mount of Saturn denotes a serious approach to life and an infallible ability to pick the right field in which to work.

Finally, the presence of a number of branches towards the Mount of Mercury indicates a wealth of intellectual, emotional and affectionate energy belonging to a person who will be much loved.

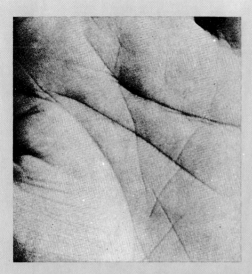

The line of Mercury is broken and interrupted, signifying considerable imagination, intuition and eccentricity. However, this person may also be subject to frequent mood changes

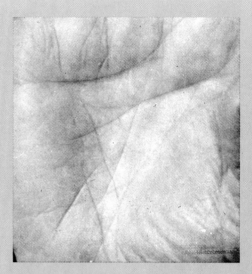

A line of Mercury, or Hepatica, originating from the life line indicates the potential for prestigious achievement. It reveals a decisive character who has sound moral sense and good judgement in decision-making

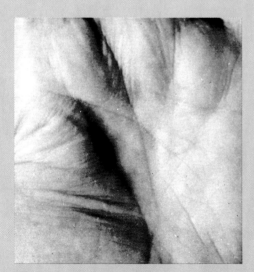

A short line of Mercury flanked by vertical lines. This reveals a dynamic person with a passion for business. Both these virtues will eventually lead to considerable success in life

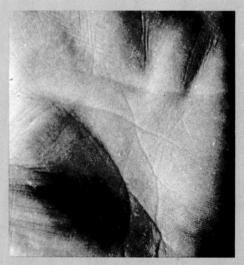

A line of Mercury formed by a number of small vertical lines drawn on the Mount of Mercury shows an individual who is prone to suffer from anxiety, nervous tension or other stress-related disorders

The line of Saturn

The line of Saturn, also known as the line of fate, belongs to the category of secondary lines. It does not have a strictly defined origin or course, and its path is sometimes confused, differing from one individual to another. To understand it better, it is necessary to consider some of its configurations.

If the line of Saturn is long and clearly defined from the base of the hand to the Mount of Saturn, this indicates a particularly fortunate characteristic; the owner is one of those people who are constantly attended by good luck. It is possible, however, that such people may have to cope with difficulties, but they will always be able to overcome them. They are industrious and have a sense of duty and an awareness of their own capabilities. They also have an enviable ability to take decisions based on logic and good sense. Constancy and thoughtfulness are two further attractive qualities, limited only by a certain tendency to avoid new experiences.

A line of Saturn that starts in the centre of the hand is an indication of adversity, particularly in the subject's youth. This will be compensated for later by material success.

A person with a fate line that starts in a fork shape has an exceptionally complex personality. The main inner conflict is between their intelligence and their perception of human nature. The 'pure' pleasures obtained from the former collide with the compromises induced by the latter.

Indecisiveness and volubility are characteristics of individuals who have a frequently interrupted fate line. The tendency towards frequent changes (in work or in life style) is a sign of a lively intellect.

When the line of Saturn starts from the heart line, this indicates that the owner's balanced outlook will ensure that he or she will always overcome problems, albeit sometimes with difficulty. Alternatively if the line starts at the head line, the head will always rule the heart and ambition and self-assurance will win these people the goals they have set themselves.

Determination and broadmindedness are the characteristics associated with a fate line that begins from the life line. This will certainly belong to a highly productive and intelligent person who is worthy of respect.

A line starting from the Mount of the Moon appears on the palms of individuals who are easily influenced. They need to develop confidence in their own judgement, beginning with relations with the opposite sex.

When the line of Saturn starts from the Mount of the Moon and shows a definite shift towards the Mount of Jupiter, this indicates a liberal, nomadic nature. Frequent travel is the *raison d'être* for such an individual. He or she will find fulfilment and economic success.

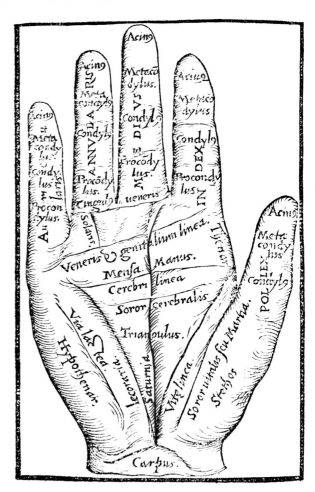

The illustration is taken from a treatise produced in the sixteenth century by Girolamo Cardano, called De Rerum Varietate Libri XVII. The line of Saturn, or fate line, is one of the least easy to identify and read as it does not have a strictly defined origin or course, and its path is often confused. A long and clearly defined fate line, as above, is a sign of good sense and indicates, too, that this person will have a particularly fortunate life

Loyalty and a good character are indicated by a line that branches either to the Mount of Saturn or to the Mount of Jupiter.

Finally, those who have a fate line running from the Mount of Venus are both attracted to and irresistible to the opposite sex. These are self-confident, brilliant and lively individuals.

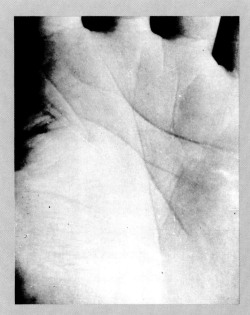

This is a long and regular line of Saturn running towards the Mount of Saturn. Obstacles in life will be happily overcome by the person concerned

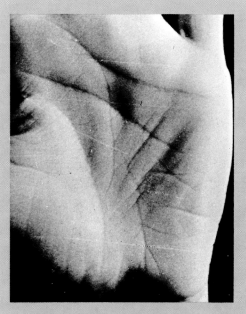

Here the line of Saturn originates in the centre of the palm. This suggests that problems will arise during life, but that they will be overcome

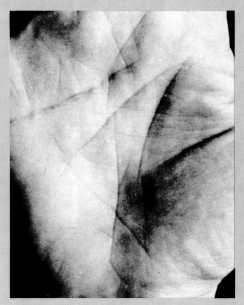

The fate line leans towards the Mount of Jupiter, and shows a desire for unusual experiences and an inclination for travel and innovation

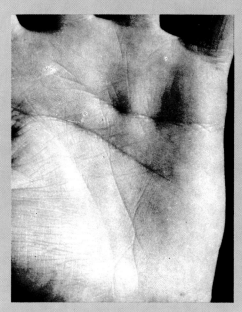

A chained line of Saturn like this is found on the hands of indecisive individuals who, despite a sense of insecurity, are determined to overcome it

3

Minor Lines

The minor lines can be difficult to recognize and interpret and so they are frequently misunderstood. These lines include the lines of marriage and children and, of course, everyone wants to know about such basic aspects of life as their marriage and the continuance of their line. However, the lines of children bear no relation to the number of offspring that the owner of the hand will produce – instead they signify unselfishness and the ability for close relationships. By the same token, the lines of travel encompass a broader meaning than just the number of voyages that will be undertaken by also revealing the owner's broadmindedness and adaptability.

The tiny lines leading from the head, life, heart and fate lines carry a wealth of meaning and you should master the interpretation of these before making any judgement on the major lines. Further indications of character come from the Plain of Mars, found in the lower central area of the palm, where the Triangle and the Quadrangle reveal the qualities of health, intelligence and sincerity.

Making a palm print is essential to mastering the science of palmistry, so this chapter also gives a simple technique for doing this.

Minor lines and marks

After considering the life line, the head line and the heart line (the principal lines), plus the lines of Apollo, Mercury and Saturn (the major secondary lines), the palmist turns to the minor secondary lines to discover the final details of the subject's personality. These minor secondary lines can sometimes be difficult to recognize.

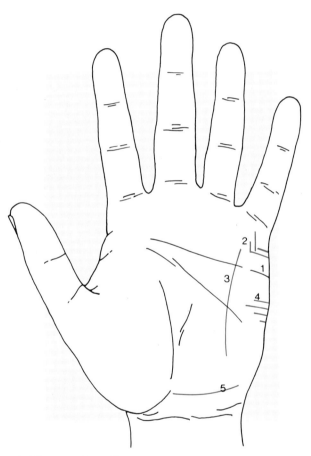

1. The marriage lines

These features are indicative of sentimental relationships and of personal relations in general, both at work and in private life. Individuals who have these lines are capable of an extraordinary depth of affection towards others. Love and generosity are the most important values to them. If a relationship or marriage appears strained, well defined lines of marriage indicate a happy solution to the problem. It was said in the past that these lines were a 'direct line to the heart, which is the source of deep feeling'.

2. The child lines

These are closely connected with the marriage lines. Altruism and commitment to others relate to the lines of children which, contrary to common belief, do not indicate the number of offspring that their owner will bring into the world. These lines express an involvement in the needs of those close to the subject, and an understanding of the meaning of life, with its highs and lows. In addition, those who have lines of sons will almost always find the strength to cope with the difficult times in life.

3. The line of intuition

The name says it all; the curve described by this feature reveals intuition, foresight and quick thinking. Premonitions derived from dreams may help the subject with decision-making. Thus the line of intuition indicates the existence of philosophical, if not religious and mystical, inclinations. It denotes sensitivity and an interest in the unsolved mysteries of life.

4. The travel lines

While these lines, as the name suggests, imply a fondness for travel, in their broader interpretation they indicate a predisposition towards change, innovation and the unusual. The owner is open-minded, flexible and adaptable when faced with the unexpected. Careful reading of the lines of travel will also reveal the number and type of moves that await the subject.

5. The Via Lasciva

Despite its name, the Via Lasciva does not indicate amorous tendencies but the level of instinctive wisdom. Loyalty, sincerity and fairmindedness are the characteristics of those who have it. Very often, the Via Lasciva expresses an unselfish nature eager to serve those less fortunate. Decisiveness and extraordinary physical health, capable of withstanding any seasonal ailments, are two more good features it indicates.

Taking a palm print

Examination of palm prints is an extremely important way of extending your understanding of the individual's character. No two palm prints are entirely similar – every individual's print is unique, to the extent that it represents a true personal 'mark'; which is why fingerprints are used as the most reliable means of identification in police and medical records.

How to make palm prints

To examine your palm prints carefully and obtain a general picture of your personality, you need first of all to fix your prints on a sheet of paper. Of the various possible methods, the simplest is to soak a wad of cotton with castor oil, smear it on to the palm of the hand and press the hand on to a sheet of porous drawing paper, 21×27 cm (8×10 inches). To maximize the clarity of the print, the paper should be placed on top of a pile of newspapers.

Oil the thumb separately, and make your thumb print in the corner of the sheet of paper.

Finally, to bring out all the large and small lines of the hand clearly, spread some manganese oxide (readily available from chemists) on to the prints.

Another method of making palm prints (and one which is particularly useful for anyone intending to collect them and review them some time later) is to blacken the palm with the kind of charcoal used by artists, then press the hand lightly but firmly on to a sheet of white paper.

It can be useful to make a collection of your own prints, and those of people of interest to you, over the years, as the formation of lines on the prints will change, faithfully following changes in character. By comparing prints from year to year, you can pick out the new factors affecting your life and personality.

Reading a palm print

The set of lines on the hand indicates the particular qualities which characterize each individual and affect the development of his or her life.

As explained in chapter 2, the three main paths that run through everyone's life are indicated by the three major basic lines – the life line, the head line and the heart line. For a comprehensive assessment of the subject's character, however, you need to establish whether the lines are wide, deep, superficial, narrow, short or long; whether they cross, are broken, chained and so on.

Broad lines

These indicate calm, reflective people who are rather slow at taking decisions, but arrive at wise ones.

Very broad lines
If the breadth is excessive, this denotes a tendency towards extravagance.

Deep lines
These are a sign of energy, physical strength and vitality.

Fine lines
These belong to people who are mindful of the quality of life and invest their energies in achieving a good life for themselves. They also reveal spontaneity, mental liveliness and a sense of self-preservation.

Superficial lines
These indicate a certain apathy and possibly a lack of energy at times.

Narrow lines
These denote a person who likes to achieve things quickly.

Long lines
The length of each line increases its specific characteristics. If a line is too long in relation to the others, this can indicate a certain imbalance (an extremely long heart line

and a short head line reveal excessive impulsiveness and extreme caution and hardheadedness respectively).

Clear, simple lines

These are easy to find in people of a serene, balanced character, especially if, in addition to being clear and simple, the lines are regular, well-drawn without interruptions, cuts or obliterations and of a good pink colour.

Very numerous lines

If the lines are dense and numerous, they indicate individuals who have considerable inner strength and possibly unusual talents, even if they are not always realized.

Broken lines

These are indicative of inconstancy and an inability to see things through.

Unclear lines

These betray inner tension and uneasiness.

Crossing lines

Lines which cut across the principal lines reveal a lack of direct personal involvement in events, however important.

Interrupted, broken lines

These show interruptions in vitality and impulsive action.

Forked lines

These indicate inner resources and hidden strengths.

Capillaried lines

These are associated with physical weakness.

Chained lines

These denote complications and lack of energy.

Sister lines

If the lines are parallel, these reveal a reinforcement of the characteristics of a given line (particularly the three principal lines of life, heart and head). It is almost as if there were an 'extra gear' provided for times of crisis. If the sister lines diverge, they denote a split personality.

Harmonious lines

These are the well-balanced lines – neither too narrow nor too broad, too faint nor too deep, too short nor too long. If truly harmonious and well-defined, their owners are people who have attained full psychological maturity, who feel at peace with themselves and with others.

A palm print taken from the hand of William Gladstone, the nineteenth-century Liberal Party leader and Prime Minister of Britain

How to tell when major events will occur

Examination of the various lines of the hand has shown that there are three principal lines (the lines of life, head and heart), plus a fourth which is almost as crucial: the line of fate (or of Saturn). Chapter 2 explains how each of these four lines relates to the length of life, the intellect, the emotions and psychological maturity respectively. However it is also possible to establish at what time in the subject's life the most important events that will affect his or her character and future will take place.

Assessing the life line

The life line is the easiest line on which to measure time. It is generally the longest and clearest line and the passage of the decades is regularly spaced along its curve.

The most traditional method is to make a palm print or draw around the hand and mark on the drawing the approximate positions of your life, head, heart and fate lines. If you trace around your hand – or use the diagram here – you will have to compare the finished drawing to your own palm. A palm print will give you a more accurate picture of the timing of events, as you will be drawing the decades of your life directly onto your own imprint. Take a pair of compasses, fix the point with the bottom of the index finger as the centre and extend the other arm to the mid-point of the base of the ring finger. Draw the arc of a circle and mark this distance on the life line. The part of the line contained between the upper side of the hand and the point thus determined will represent the first 10 years of your life. Then extend the movable arm to the division between the ring finger and the little finger, draw another arc and the distance between the two points on the life line will be your life between the ages of 10 and 20. The movable arm extended to the mid point of the little finger, the tip of the hand and the base of the little finger and the percussion of the palm where it crosses the heart line, will give the ages of 30, 40 and 50 respectively.

Then measure the percussion of the hand under the heart line – two thirds along the distance between the base of the little finger and that line – extend the compass to this point, and mark the distance relating to 60 years on the life line. For the following decades, take two thirds of the distance given by the previous decade.

The years are thus read in descending order on the life line from top to bottom (see diagram). The longer the line, the greater the certainty of long life *should* be. However, in reality a short line does not necessarily indicate a short life. It has, in fact, been found quite frequently that a short line will lengthen over the years. The will to live, coupled with effort put into taking care of the health, can extend a person's life and hence, as a reflex, extend the life line on the palm of the hand.

A short line is, in any event, interpreted as a lack of energy and a weak constitution. This condition can remain stable, improve or worsen depending on how the subject reacts to this handicap. Remember that the short line, to indicate a lack of vitality, must appear the same on both hands. In fact, the short life line often appears only on the left hand, which relates to hereditary conditions, and is longer on the right hand, indicating the desire for a long life.

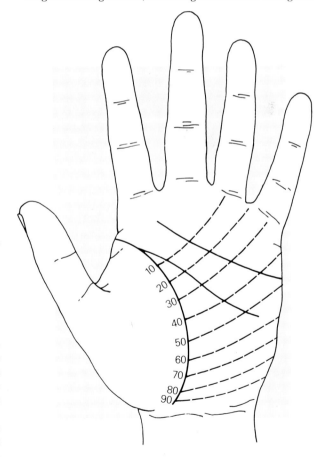

The palmar timepiece: the calculation has been worked out on the life line in decades, shown at the intersections of the dotted lines

A long and well-defined life line, is however, a favourable sign and augurs well for a long life spent in good health. If there are interruptions along it, these betoken a risk of illness (although the interruption, to be of any concern, must appear on both hands). The point at which this interruption appears tells you approximately the age at which the illness is likely to occur.

If the interruption is flanked by parallel lines on both hands, this is a reassuring sign; it means that the owner has hidden reserves that will come to his or her aid at critical moments.

If the interruption bends towards the thumb, this means that the illness is liable to become chronic. In this case, at the relevant age at which the interruption is shown on the palm, the subject must try as far as possible to prevent this chronic condition from occurring.

If the life line is interrupted by small transverse lines, this means that at these periods in the subject's life his or her vitality and health will be disturbed by nervous complaints. These psychological disorders will be more serious if they are shown at the start of the line (in youth) or towards the end (in old age).

Assessing the head line

Unlike the life line, in which the passage of the decades is regularly spaced along its curve, the head line shows the stages in longer sections between the ages of 10 and 30, then closer together from 30 to 50 and beyond. This is because the most important events relating to intellectual development and to the formation of the personality take place in the first 30 years.

Breaks are therefore of greater concern in this first section, and indicate the presence of psychological conflicts, emotional traumas, disagreements with parents and any factors that are liable to interfere with the normal development of the intelligence and creativity with which everyone is endowed.

If, following breaks in the first part, the head line then continues to the end more clearly, cleanly and deeply, this means that the subject has been able to overcome all mental conflicts in maturity.

Assessing the heart line

In assessing the sections of the heart line, too, you should bear in mind that the first 30 to 40 years are well spaced out, while from 40 upwards the decades appear closer together. The reason for this is that the love life has a greater wealth of ups and downs in the first and second stages of life. The interruptions that appear in the section relating to the first 30 years indicate, step by step, the anxiety and pain caused by broken love affairs, separations and stress. If the interruption is particularly clear, this can also indicate organic heart troubles which to some extent can be caused by emotional stress.

Assessing the line of Saturn

The line of Saturn indicates the timing of events with well-spaced stages from 10 to 30 years, condensing the next 40 to 50 years in the final part (see diagram).

Here again, the reason is that we build our own destiny in the first 30 years of life, formulating our own way of thinking and acting from the values of the society in which we live.

If the line of Saturn is interrupted around the age of 20 to 30, this means that the subject has failed to use his or her potential qualities to full advantage. But the line of Saturn, like the life line, can lengthen over the years. Whether or not it does will depend on how much ambition is stimulated.

Interruptions indicate difficulties in seeing projects through. If the last part of the line of Saturn is still clear and well-defined, this means that difficulties will be overcome and that the recognition and achievements which were missing in the first half of life will in due course come.

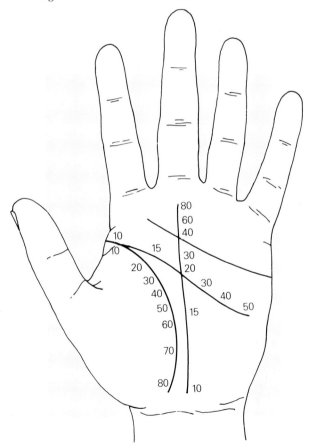

This diagram shows periods of time in decades on the life, head, heart and fate lines. Use it as a basis for analysing periods of life on your palm

The Plain of Mars

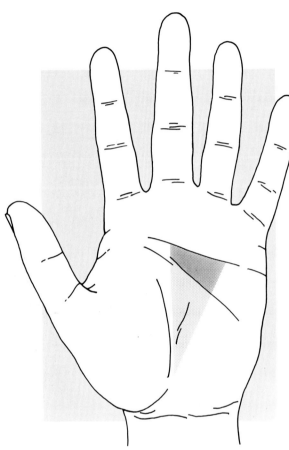

The areas occupied by the two parts of the Plain of Mars: the Quadrangle and the Triangle

The name 'Plain of Mars' is given to the part of the palm that descends from the centre (at the level of the Mount of Mars) almost to the wrist. The Plain of Mars is subdivided into two parts: the Quadrangle and the Triangle, so called because of the geometric shapes that they form.

The Quadrangle, contained between the heart line and the head line, indicates the degree of sincerity and goodness.

The Triangle, located between the life line and the head line, reveals the degree of intelligence and health.

The Quadrangle

Large and broad
This is a sign of an open, loyal and strong character.

Excessively large
This indicates tactlessness; courage goes beyond bravery and verges upon foolhardiness.

Narrow
This is indicative of a tendency to lie and betray. It is also a sign of possible cardiac disorders.

Marked by a circle
This shows hypersensitivity and weak vision.

Marked by a cross
This reveals a bent for the spiritual life.

Marked by various small lines
This betrays a weak character, who is influenced by others and cannot form his or her own opinions.

Marked by a star
Such a hand shows marked intuition and psychic powers.

Marked by a definite spot
This character will be nervous and apt to suffer from respiratory disorders.

The Triangle

Large and well-defined
A generous nature, good psycho-physical balance, excellent intellectual powers and tiptop health are indicated by this Triangle.

Very long
This individual has an altruistic spirit and great sensitivity and will use his or her intelligence to achieve great ideals.

Narrow
In this subject intellectual potential is limited, partly due to a narrow mind. He or she will fail out of fear of taking on ambitious commitments that could change his or her life.

Marked by a small circle
This denotes an aggressive, voluble character.

Marked by a cross
This indicates restlessness that brings complications and conflicts in both family and professional relations.

Marked by a star
A star indicates a combative nature; this person will be determined to impose his or her views on others.

Marked by a black spot
This denotes a weakness in the health. However, this person has inner resources and will overcome the illness and make a speedy recovery.

Marked by a blemish
Possible disorders of the liver and a tendency to anger are indicated.

The illustration opposite is from Ludicrum Chiromanticum

What the lines reveal about happiness in marriage

The American Palmistry Enthusiasts' Club, with its headquarters in Washington and branches in New York, Detroit, Reno and San Francisco, has more than 14,000 members. In addition to a series of elegantly furnished offices and restaurants (the New York branch even has a discotheque), members also have the use of a rich and unusual library. This houses manuals and books on palmistry from all over the world and in a wide range of languages that they are able to consult *in situ*, or at home if they have been members for a year or more. One of the books in the library asks, 'Are you sure that you are a good husband?' This illustrated book, entitled *Sex and palmistry*, is one of the books most frequently consulted by the public. Examples on the opposite page come from the book.

Cupid and Psyche *by Antonio Canova, the eighteenth-century Italian sculptor and painter who sought to create a new and purified classicism*

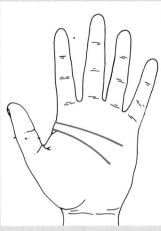

Left
When the heart and head lines are well-defined and very wide apart, this indicates a great ability to love and be loved

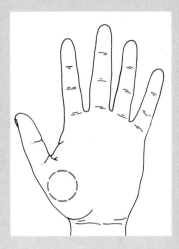

Right
A well-defined and well-developed Mount of Venus shows very strong sexual desires and emotional openness

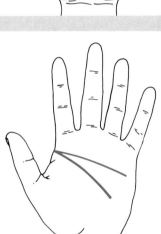

Left
Heart and head lines touching and appearing to start almost from the same point suggest that difficulties may arise in love

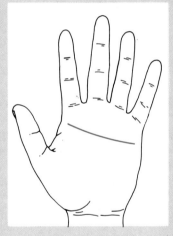

Right
A heart line curved at its end can indicate an aggressive and selfish person who is unable to distinguish between love and sex

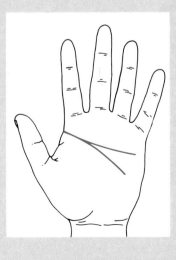

Left
Where heart and head lines meet and overlap the person concerned may tend to overlook the needs of his or her partner for life

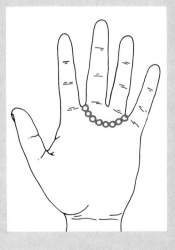

Right
A dense, well-defined girdle of Venus reveals an unfaithful partner who would do well to mend his or her ways

4

The Mounts

The seven fleshy protuberances on the palm of the hand are known as mounts, each one associated with a planet whose qualities it symbolizes. Considered on their own, they may not hold a great deal of significance but the lines and marks on them make them vitally important in establishing the character of the subject.

Of the seven mounts, Venus represents emotional and sexual love; Jupiter, strength of character; Saturn, wisdom and ambition; Apollo, artistic and aesthetic sense; Mercury, intelligence, versatility and practicality; Mars, courage, assertiveness and physical and mental strength; and the Moon, imagination, sensuality and romanticism. The latter mount is not easy to read but it is worth mastering because it is the most revealing of the mounts as to the core of your subject's character. Saturn, although classified with the mounts, differs from the others in that it is quite concave in form.

Following these precepts, you might expect to find a well-developed Mount of Mars on the hand of a military person; a businessman might show you a high Mount of Mercury, while an artist would certainly possess a larger-than-average Mount of Apollo. Remember that, as usual, the characteristic must be evident in both hands.

The Mount of Venus

This is the most obvious and important mount, found at the base of the thumb. Depending on the shape, the thickness and the signs that cross it, it is possible to establish the extent to which the subject has the qualities of vitality, good-naturedness and instinctive sexuality.

Large and well-defined
This indicates considerable energy and well-balanced sensuality. Individuals who have a well-formed Mount of Venus know how to create true warmth of affection within the family and have artistic qualities, particularly in the fields of music, painting, dance and sculpture.

Over-developed
When the Mount of Venus is excessively prominent and is considerably larger than all the other mounts in the palm, this reveals a hot temperament, its owner being inclined to allow himself or herself to be carried away by sensuality. This person is often restless, unfaithful and foolish. If the rest of the hand looks harmonious, however, the eroticism is more imaginary than real.

Under-developed
This belongs to a person of little vitality and of controlled feelings. In these individuals, reason prevails over impulse.

Broad
This denotes a sound and robust physical constitution, a happy and passionate character.

Very narrow
If this type of Mount of Venus belongs to a woman, it indicates certain psychological or physical difficulties with sex. On the palm of a man, it may indicate limited sexual potency, or extreme prudence in amorous relationships.

Towards the centre of the palm
This denotes a firm and decisive character. These people know how to make the best use of their energies, dividing them between important professional activities and a passionate sex life.

Low or flat
This means that the individual has a somewhat cold and lethargic character. Little sex drive may perhaps be due to poor health or to inhibitions.

Almost non-existent
These people have a weak, childish and egotistical temperament. They do not know how to enjoy life, and are insecure.

Hard or soft
A hard Mount of Venus indicates an aggressive and overbearing character. In a harmonious hand, this may be limited to a quest for power and success. In a non-harmonious hand, it can express brutality in sexual relations. If it is very soft, the Mount of Venus reveals a passive, weak, over-sexed character.

A protruding lower part
This type of elevation denotes marked artistic tendencies into which the person to some extent sublimates his or her sexual energies.

Marked by a star
If a star appears on the Mount of Venus, this means that the individual is undergoing, or has undergone, an important experience in the field of love. If there is more than one star, this is a person of many loves!

Chained
Chained lines on the Mount of Venus indicate a tendency on the part of the subject to tie himself or herself in the wrong relationships, friendships and marriages.

Crosses
A single cross on the Mount of Venus indicates individuals who devote themselves to a single great love. A number of crosses denotes a confused love life, which is a possible source of complications.

Grilles
Grilles on the Mount of Venus are typical of individuals who heighten their own eroticism with fantasies. They also indicate marked creativity and artistic flair and an ability to overcome all difficulties with clever solutions.

Horizontal lines
These indicate difficulties in achieving a happy love life as a result of inhibitions and rigid morals.

Vertical lines
When the Mount of Venus is crossed by vertical lines, the individual is sexually balanced and lives in a healthy and instinctive manner.

The Mount of Jupiter

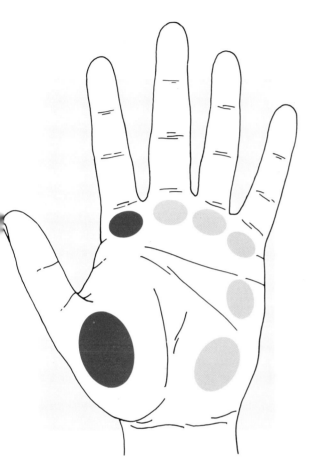

Of the seven mounts, this is possibly the most important for determining strength of character at a glance.

Well-developed
This is characteristic of people who believe in ideals and battle for them without accepting any compromise.

Over-prominent
This is considered as such when the prominence extends so far as to occupy a large part of the middle finger. In this case, it reveals a tendency towards vanity, bossiness and egocentricity. This person is strong and tenacious, capable of arousing awe with the enthusiasm with which every action is undertaken and with their absence of self-doubt.

Hollow
If the Mount of Jupiter is absent or downright hollow, the individual is depressed, passive and resigned, with few interests of his or her own.

Swollen and hard
The qualities of sincerity and goodness are pronounced. These people are perhaps a little prone to elaborate speeches, but they genuinely try to fulfil their ideals.

Normal
An average-sized Mount of Jupiter reveals a calm and well-balanced character and attachment to the family.

Pointing towards the heart line
This indicates an energetic, passionate temperament with a great deal of self-esteem and a touch of narcissism.

Pointing towards the life line
This denotes a deep bond with the individual's parents and relatives. He or she values traditions and education.

Pointing towards the head line
These people's ambitions are in the field of arts and intellect, for which they are admirably suited.

Marked by a star
A favourable sign that indicates decisive people, capable of implementing their own projects. If, however, there is more than one star, these people tend to be self-satisfied and in the race for success may overlook spiritual values.

Marked by a diagonal cross
This is the 'Cross of St Andrew' which indicates a person whose heart favours happy relationships. Two or three diagonal crosses also reveal great enthusiasm and initiative.

Straight cross
This denotes an ambitious character who will seek out people of high status and salary. This also extends to their marriage partners!

Grille
This is typical of people who lead a very busy or disorganized life, which makes the achievement of major projects difficult.

Circle
This reveals a tendency towards perfection. It is found in people who are able to achieve success purely on their own merits.

Chains
These are characteristic of people who complicate their lives with anxieties and fears – although, in the end, they will generally come out on top.

Small vertical lines
This is the sign that reveals a social climber of considerable tenacity!

Small horizontal lines
These reveal a relatively unimaginative character, but one who is capable of slowly progressing towards his or her objective. This person is strong-willed.

The Mount of Saturn

The Mount of Saturn is located at the base of the middle finger. The middle finger represents restrictions, duty and hard work. The Mount of Saturn is generally not as prominent as the other mounts, so that a well-developed Mount of Saturn will be relatively flat compared to the other mounts.

Many great thinkers – and many great saints – have a particularly well-developed Mount of Saturn, but so too have many men of action. Napoleon Bonaparte had a well-defined Mount of Saturn, as does Fidel Castro today.

Well-developed
If it is neither too prominent nor too flattened, it indicates that the person is fairminded and able to organize his or her life well. People who have this Mount of Saturn are likely, sooner or later, to achieve their goals. Their state of health is good.

Over-developed
This is seen in people who allow themselves to be overtaken by events, which may lead to their being bitter and mistrustful misogynists: they may become depressed, solitary, introverted and egocentric, hate to show affection and even find it hard to love.

Flat or hollow
This indicates a tendency to escape duties and responsibilities. It is seen in those who would like an independent, sometimes extravagant life, but who do not have sufficiently clear ideas as to how to achieve it. According to medical palmistry, the absence of a Mount of Saturn reveals constitutional weakness.

Soft and low
This is typical of conformist, disorganized people with no enthusiasm or ideals.

Pointing towards the base of the ring finger
This denotes a strong character capable of shaking off social conditioning and achieving personal goals. It is characteristic of artists, dreamers and optimists.

Marked with a cross
Attraction towards the occult, mysticism and paranormal phenomena is associated with this sign. It sometimes reveals uncommon qualities of clairvoyance and most frequently belongs to those with a psychic hand shape.

Marked with a star
This denotes a rebellious character who may be involved in scandals as a result of his or her lack of caution. Such a person often has a dramatic fate.

Marked with a triangle
This indicates considerable intuition, wisdom and spirituality. This person strives for perfection and harmony. He or she may be interested in the occult.

Marked with a square
This reveals an ability to defend oneself against dangers and enemies.

Marked with small vertical lines
This reveals a strong person, one who follows a straight path to reach ambitious objectives and has a sense of his or her own worth.

Marked with small horizontal lines
This indicates that the person does not know how to react to difficulties and may ultimately accept events passively; he or she is unlikely to be materially successful. It is also a sign of inhibition and timidity.

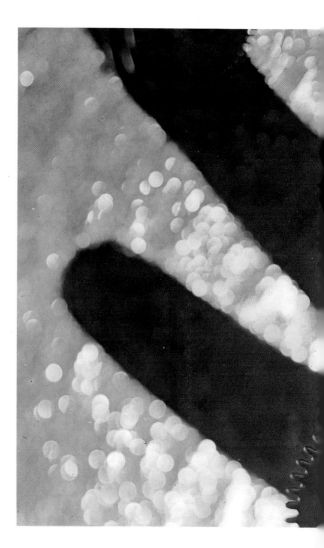

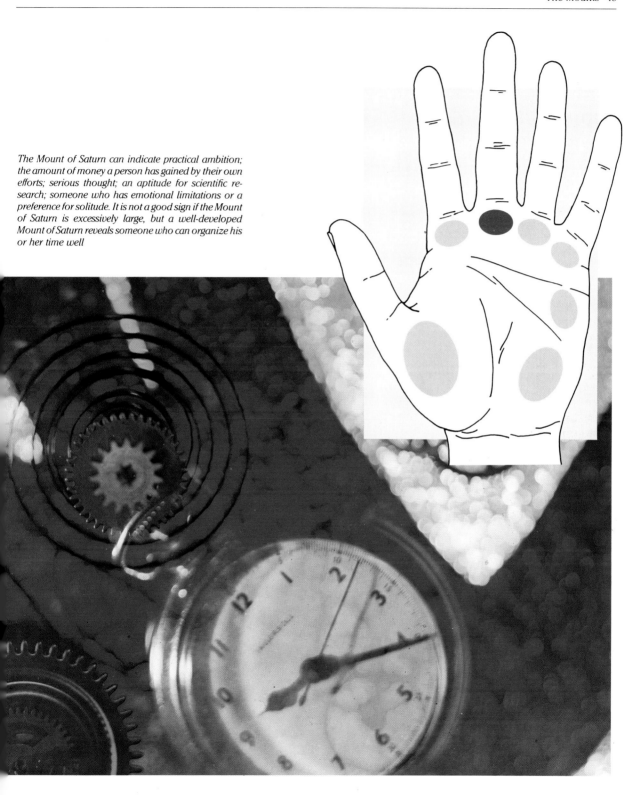

The Mount of Saturn can indicate practical ambition; the amount of money a person has gained by their own efforts; serious thought; an aptitude for scientific research; someone who has emotional limitations or a preference for solitude. It is not a good sign if the Mount of Saturn is excessively large, but a well-developed Mount of Saturn reveals someone who can organize his or her time well

The Mount of Apollo

The Mount of Apollo is located at the base of the ring finger. It is a slightly fleshy protrusion which, according to its form, reveals whether its owner possesses artistic or creative qualities, aesthetic taste and sensitivity.

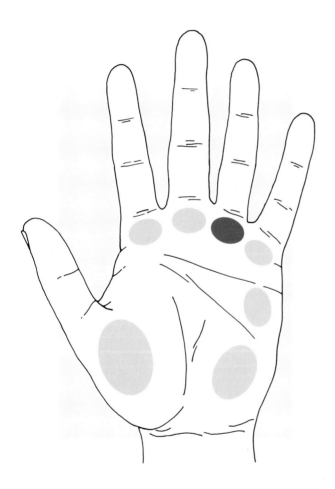

This diagram shows the exact location of the Mount of Apollo which, according to its size, reveals the amount of artistic talent its owner has. If it is too large, however, the person will be self-satisfied and – resting on his or her laurels – may cease to strive for the necessary perfection to improve his or her talents. Socially those with a normally developed Mount of Apollo project themselves well and attract others with their witty and engaging conversation

Well-pronounced
This indicates an ability to express particular talents in the artistic field – painting, music, poetry, and literature. Such people love nature and everything that is beautiful, har-

monious and aesthetically perfect. In addition they are often gifted with lucid expression and make brilliant conversationalists.

Over-developed

If the Mount of Apollo is disproportionately large in relation to the other mounts of the hand, this means that the owner is altogether too pleased with his or her artistic qualities. This self-congratulation will impair the ability for

objective self-criticism, ultimately lowering this person's standards. Vanity will also jeopardize his or her love life. A craving for material possessions can complicate his or her economic situation, as this person has a tendency to spend beyond his or her means. In medical palmistry, an over-developed Mount of Apollo indicates possible sight defects and heart disorders.

Flat or depressed

This is a characteristic of timid or introverted people who do not have any particular artistic talents or who, if they do have any, ultimately suffocate them. At times this is caused by harsh self-criticism.

Extending to the base of the middle finger

This means that the owner's artistic capabilities are enhanced by study and contemplation. It is typical of artists who devote themselves seriously to their profession and prefer to be engrossed in their work rather than concentrate on their status. It can also be a sign of philosophical interests.

Extending to the base of the little finger

These people have artistic qualities that are put to practical use. This is a characteristic that belongs to art dealers, painters, actors and musicians who aim to achieve riches and popular success in a hurry.

Extending beneath the middle finger and little finger

This denotes the complete artist who knows how to balance the aesthetic aspect of art with its economic realities. It is a typical characteristic of those who do everything themselves – actors, authors, directors and producers, for example.

Marked with a star

This reveals an unbridled desire to show off! The star is often seen in people who peak suddenly in their careers but enjoy only a brief success.

Marked with a triangle

If the triangle is well-defined, this indicates true brilliance and talent.

Marked with a grille

This is typical of people who have potential artistic talent, but who lack the discipline or the motivation to use it in a constructive way.

Marked with a cross

These people lack self-confidence and so do not make the most of their artistic talents.

Marked with a square

The subject's artistic bent is balanced by self-control and level-headedness. Such people are capable of defending themselves from envy, enmity and rivalry. They do not waste time in day dreaming.

Marked with a spot

If the spot is obvious and deep, it indicates a tendency to throw oneself into artistic pursuits too easily at the risk of failure to complete them. If the spot is white, it can reveal problems with the sight.

The Mount of Mercury

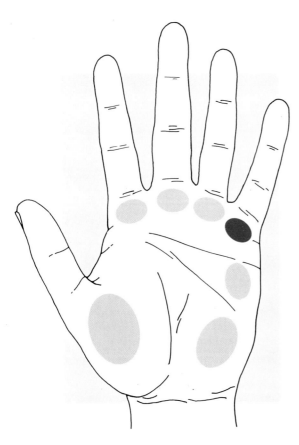

The Mount of Mercury consists of a slightly fleshy protrusion at the base of the little finger. This mount reveals the qualities symbolically attributed to Mercury: intelligence, practicality, communicability, eloquence, versatility and astuteness.

Well-proportioned

When the protrusion under the little finger is pronounced and well-proportioned in relation to the other mounts in the hand, it indicates a rational, realistic, sociable character with an aptitude for science or medicine. In general, this feature is found in people who have done well financially thanks to brilliant ideas or inventions.

Over-developed

When the protrusion extends beyond the other mounts, this means that the owner is arrogant and uses his or her astuteness and intelligence for monetary gain and personal convenience. These individuals will follow almost any avenue in order to obtain economic or professional success in a hurry. They have a passion for travel and adventure and an ability to fascinate others with their sexual magnetism and tall tales. In medical palmistry this characteristic denotes a tendency to nervous exhaustion.

Flat

This indicates a poor practical sense and a somewhat apathetic character. This person is not good with money and does not shine in company.

Low and soft

This betokens an introvert with a routine life style. His or her interests are limited, and in choice of lovers he or she lacks imagination.

Non-existent

This person is naive, somewhat slow on the uptake and easily deceived.

Prominent mount on the percussion

A prominent mount on the edge of the hand indicates extreme astuteness and a craving for money. Greed may possibly lead to fraud or theft.

Extending towards the base of the ring finger

This denotes an ability to combine business sense with aesthetic taste. It is typical of people who know how to make money from their artistic abilities.

Marked with a star

This reveals great ability in the commercial field and considerable astuteness. At times, the owner may resort to trickery in order to profit materially.

Marked with a cross

Again, greed may drive the owner to unscrupulous methods.

Marked with a square

This denotes an ability to weather the dangers of an extremely adventurous life. Even at most difficult moments, this individual will find a way out.

Marked with various radii

This indicates an intelligent, impulsive person with a considerable ability to influence others.

Marked with a spot

This reveals a strong leaning towards illegal dealings. However, if the spot is combined with a square on the mount, this is cancelled out.

Marked with a grille

This means that the owner has little confidence in himself or herself, and is not always able to close business deals effectively.

Marked with a triangle

This shows a lively mind and a good grasp of business affairs. Its owner has the potential for prosperity and personal achievement.

The Mount of Mars

The Mount of Mars is located just under the Mount of Mercury (which is found at the base of the little finger), exactly between the lines of heart and head, extending as far as the percussion (the side of the hand). This mount reveals the 'martial' qualities – courage, combative spirit, physical energy, strength to cope with the adversities of life and strong passions.

Well-developed
This indicates a strong and aggressive character capable of overcoming every obstacle. These people have such physical and mental energy that they are never discouraged and can always find new solutions to problems. They are industrious by nature and they will take the lead, in both their professional and personal life, in moments of difficulty.

Excessively protuberant
If the Mount of Mars protrudes more than the other mounts to a disproportionate extent, this reveals an argumentative and quarrelsome nature. These people are violent, foolhardy and extremely competitive. If obstacles are put in their way, they will even indulge in acts of cruelty. In medical palmistry it denotes a risk of heart attack, infarct, laryngitis, bronchitis.

Relatively under-developed
This reveals a submissive person who allows himself or herself to be dominated by others. These individuals do not try to improve their lot but resign themselves to their situation.

Low and soft
This indicates a calm, conciliatory temperament. Such people will only assert their rights in moments of exceptional exasperation.

Virtually non-existent
These subjects are weak, timid and cowardly. Physically, they may lack resistance to fatigue and stress.

Extending to the head line
This strong, combative character also possesses considerable intellectual powers and is able to use his or her energies to a good end.

Extending vertically towards the wrist
This reveals physical and mental power. This person is able to impose his or her will in a virtually hypnotic fashion.

Marked by a cross
This denotes an aggressive and possessive temperament. In love, these people may have love-hate relationships of such passion that they verge on the melodramatic.

Marked by a triangle
This shows an energetic and disciplined person who may reach a high rank in the armed forces or who excels in the organization of ventures that require courage and dedication.

Marked by small lines
This indicates excessive foolhardiness which can lead to dangerous undertakings. These people are so determined to demonstrate their courage that they expose themselves to serious risks.

Marked by a star
This denotes intelligence and self-control. The owners may achieve positions of command in both military and civilian life. Their courage is short-sighted and as a result frequently harmful.

Marked by a square
This indicates a person who rarely takes risks or impulsive decisions. At most he or she may take a calculated risk.

Marked by a grille
This denotes a strong, possibly violent, nature.

No small lines or marks
This belongs to a person who relies on courage and sangfroid. The mount must, however, be pronounced and in proportion with the rest of the hand.

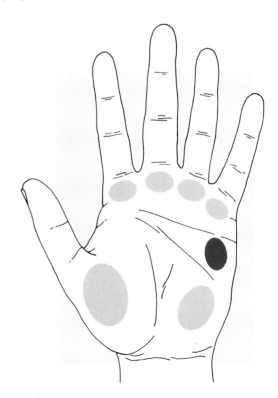

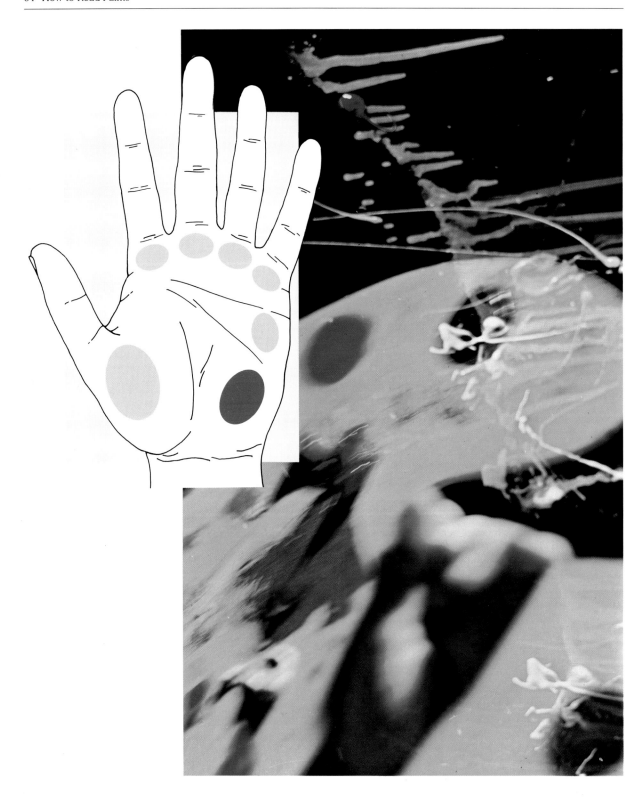

The Mount of the Moon

The Mount of the Moon is located under the Mount of Mars, just above the wrist and below the little finger. It is a fleshy protrusion that takes in the percussion of the hand (the edge) and reveals the 'lunar' characteristics of the personality – fantasy, imagination, volubility, the tendency to romanticize and curiosity. When fully developed it indicates the desire to accept, and be accepted by, all levels of society, and also the longing to travel. A smaller mount means these tendencies are reduced.

Normally developed

If the mount appears along the edge of the hand and is well proportioned in relation to the other mounts, it means that the subject has pronounced emotions and imagination. He or she is inquisitive, intuitive, and full of private desires that often remove him or her from the real world to one of dreams and ideals. This is an impressionable, poetic and gently melancholic character with a leaning towards sentimental infatuations for the opposite sex.

Excessively developed

If this mount exhibits a greater bulge than the others, forming a cushion at the bottom of the hand, it means that the owner's imagination is so vivid that it borders upon the visionary or hallucinatory. Such people are liable to live in a dream world, mythicizing themselves and everything about them. This bulge is also a sign of gluttony, sensuality and personal magnetism. In medical palmistry it denotes a predisposition to gout, dropsy, kidney and bladder disorders.

Under-developed

This is a calm and realistic character who does not like to extend the restricted circle of his or her interests and affections. He or she will have poor aesthetic sense and controlled, and sometimes cold, feelings.

Low and flat

This is typical of individuals who are somewhat pedantic and fixed in their ways and do not like the unexpected. They also dislike any sentimentalism or romantic impulses, regarding them as a danger to their set way of life.

Virtually non-existant

The owners of such a hand are self-contained and self-centred, refusing all romantic relationships. Hypochondria, fear and emotional sterility make them very isolated.

With a prominent centre

This denotes difficulty in distinguishing between the imagination and reality. These subjects are egocentric, obsessive, but also inventive. They have a good memory.

Extending upwards

This shows an imaginative ability which may come to fruition in literary or musical creation. This person has unusual qualities and, even if a dreamer, will struggle to make his or her mark in society.

Extending towards the Mount of Venus

This shows that the imagination relates above all to erotic, romantic and fantastic adventures.

Marked with a cross

This reveals a tendency to tell tall stories and to claim non-existent successes and conquests. It may also indicate strong mystical or religious leanings.

Marked with a star

This indicates a romantic character with a strong attraction for travel to far-distant countries with adventurous journeys on the way over exotic seas and unexplored lands.

Marked with a grille

This betrays too much imagination which causes nervousness and tension, making practical achievements difficult for this subject.

Marked with a square

This person usually has his or her feet firmly on the ground.

Marked with a spot

This denotes a strong craving to escape the daily grind and avoid routine tasks.

Marked with a triangle

This indicates psychic gifts and clairvoyance.

Marked with an island

This reveals the subject's ability to isolate himself or herself in an imaginary world and to create something unusual in the artistic field.

5

Fingers and Nails

The shape and form of the fingers have played an important role in both ancient and modern palmistry – the palmists of old, for example, used to read the fortunes of adolescents in the index finger! The fingers represent the more instinctive facets of the character, while the palm is held to indicate the subject's practical qualities.

Look at the fingers separately and collectively from the front and back to determine their individual appearance and their relationship to each other. In establishing the length of the fingers, the yardstick of average length is that the middle finger should be within three-quarters to seven-eighths of the length of the palm.

Each finger is divided into three phalanges, which you should consider in relation to each other as well as to the corresponding phalange on the other fingers. The shape of the nails on the first phalange, for example, may not be constant from finger to finger.

The colour and strength of the nails, the appearance of the moons and any blemishes that are present are pointers not only to personality but also to the subject's state of physical health and, possibly, to the quality of his or her diet.

The fingers and nails

The shape of the fingers

The basic shape of the fingers can reveal a good deal about the subject's character. The different shapes and their significance are as follows:

Long
These indicate intelligence.
Short
Short fingers show impulsiveness.
Wide
A conscientious person, but lacking great intelligence.
Square
A careful, thoughtful person.
Spatulate
An active, dynamic person.
Girdled
A kind, altruistic person.
Tapered
An artistic, impulsive, but also meticulous nature.
Thin
An introverted individual with a strong aesthetic sense.
Short and thick
These reveal pronounced egotism.
Curved
A sign of ill-will and a hot temper.
Fleshy
These point to hedonism and narcissim.
Smooth joints
Impulsiveness in both action and thought.
Knotty joints
Depth of thought, nobility of spirit.
Thick joints
A rational, analytical and methodical mind.

The shape of the nails

Short nails
Short nails are indicative of an active, curious and intuitive nature.
Short, broad nails
When broad as well as short, nails show a critical sense and impulsiveness.
Long, wide and rounded nails
These reveal a person endowed with a balanced judgement.
Long, almond-shaped nails
This is the distinctive feature of the romantic dreamer and reveals a placid, good-natured individual.
Broad, square nails
Coldness, egotism and determination are indicated.
Wedge-shaped nails
These show marked sensitivity in the individual and an even temperament.

The colour of the nails

White
The owner is characterized by coldness, presumptiveness and cynicism.
Pale pink
This person has a jovial and expansive nature and enjoys all kinds of social events.
Red
These are the nails of someone with a fiery, violent and sanguine nature.
Violet blue
This is a sign of poor health.

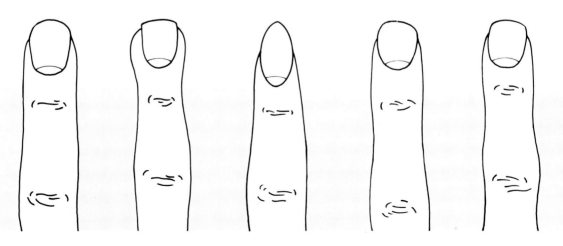

The base joints of the fingers

The base joint of the middle finger is the highest and so it is this finger that is used to establish the level at which the other fingers join the palm of the hand.

Base joints at the same level

This is typical of a person endowed with a great deal of good sense and a positive nature, who is destined to succeed in life.

Base joints at different levels

This is the most common type of hand. Life will be adventurous, full of surprises, highs and lows.

Base joints at a lower level than that of the middle finger

This reveals a shy person who finds it difficult to assert himself or herself but who, on better acquaintance, turns out to be well worth knowing.

Ring finger lower than the middle

This is found in people who are frustrated in their career, having taken a job to which they are not suited.

Little finger lower than the middle

This denotes an individual who will have to fight hard to succeed and will never be handed anything on a plate.

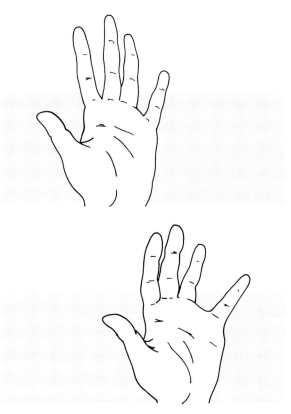

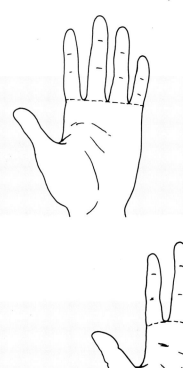

Arrangement of the fingers

Fingers close together

This indicates caution, suspicion, lack of sociability.

Regularly spaced fingers

This person has a balanced mentality and will succeed in whichever field he or she chooses.

Fingers well separated

This denotes an independent, freedom-loving spirit.

Considerable space between the fingers

This indicates a sincere, open and trustworthy nature.

Large space between the thumb and index finger

This is an extrovert character, predisposed towards generosity.

Index and middle finger well separated

This person is endowed with independent thought and action and is not easily influenced.

Space between the middle finger and ring finger

This is typical of a person who is not troubled by worries of the future but lives for today.

Ring finger and little finger well separated

This indicates an original and imaginative thinker.

Little finger well separated from the other fingers

This person is diffident and isolated and has difficulties in relationships with others.

The index finger

Once you have mastered the significance of the general appearance of the hand and the meaning of the lines and mounts on the palm it is time to move on to the individual fingers.

The index finger was known in ancient times as the digit of Jupiter. Jupiter is the planet that symbolizes wisdom, good sense, generosity and optimism. Above all, it is the planet of justice – hence you use the index finger to stress what you feel to be correct, or to accuse those whom you believe to be wrong.

For some people, the index finger is the finger of clairvoyance: it is in fact this finger that you use to point out things in the distance and metaphorically it points to targets that you seek to attain. The index finger is also the 'teacher's finger': no doubt you remember having seen your teachers raise it to emphasize their points.

More than any other digit, the index finger, placed against the thumb, enables you to assess the texture or consistency of a fabric or of a small object. It is thus the 'finger of sensitivity'.

It is important to compare the length of each phalange with those on the other fingers for an overall character assessment. There are many meanings attributed to the shape and length of this finger and the following are the main ones recognized in modern palmistry.

Long
This belongs to ambitious individuals who know how to achieve practical and economic aims. It is also a sign of self-assurance and certainty.

Short
This reveals a lack of self-confidence and, possibly, a sense of inferiority also, which renders self-assertion more difficult. If the thumb is short as well as the index finger, there may be a sense of frustration that can cause health problems such as hypertension or ulcers.

Longer than the ring finger
This reveals a desire for affluence, pleasure and comfort. It is a characteristic of people who like to give orders and who wish to achieve important positions.

Longer than the middle finger
This person has to guard against arrogance and aggression to achieve success. The desire to win and to be noticed can also make him or her snobbish and unsympathetic towards other people. What counts most for this person is his or her career.

Average length
When the index finger reaches to the middle of the first phalange of the middle finger, it may be regarded as normal. This belongs to people who know how to manage their lives and who always find the right solution to their problems. They are proud and ambitious, but they also take account of the needs of others.

Pointed
This is often found in people who have acute powers of observation and enjoy intellectual pursuits. When the pointed finger is also very long this signifies fastidiousness, fanaticism and a tendency to be hypercritical.

A perfectly rounded tip
This reveals a tendency to eliminate conflict and to round off the sharp edges of incompatibility. It also denotes an ability to control impulse and to enter into pleasant friendships.

Curved
This is a sign of intelligence but also of a lack of diplomacy and prudence, as a result of which the owner is liable to encounter obstacles in social and professional relationships. He or she lacks a sense of proportion.

Very long first phalange
When the first phalange of the index finger (the one with the nail) is longer than the other two, it reveals sensitivity and a predisposition towards respiratory disorders.

Very long second phalange
If the middle phalange of the index finger is longer than the other two, this indicates dynamism, efficiency and enterprise. It is a typical characteristic of an active person and, in particular, of a good surgeon.

Very long third phalange
The last phalange of the index finger (the lowest phalange), if greater in length than the other two, indicates tenacity in implementing projects. If this phalange tends to lengthen or widen, it reveals a predisposition towards rheumatic disorders, gout and liver disorders.

Short first phalange
This reveals a materialistic person with little faith in human nature.

Short second phalange
Those with a short second phalange are usually unambitious.

Short third phalange
If the last phalange of the index finger is short, it reveals someone who deals with mundane tasks easily and capably.

Thin first phalange
If the phalange with the nail is thin it suggests that this person is rather inflexible and likes to go by the book.

Thin second phalange
This denotes an ambitious subject who cannot easily

Michelangelo's The Creation of Adam *in the Sistine Chapel, Rome*

be restrained.
Thin third phalange
This person is an aesthete, but also very conventional.
Very incisive vertical grooves
These are thin, vertical lines which, when pronounced, indicate a loyal person who has a serious and dedicated approach to work.

An index fingerprint
Try putting some ink or cold wax on the first phalange of the index finger and making a print on a sheet of white paper. If the lines are arched, this means that you are of a nervous nature, predisposed to exhaustion. If there is a wealth of convolutions or vortices, your body is sound, balanced and resistant to physical and mental ills.

The middle finger

Of all the fingers, those valuable indicators of the character and intellect, the middle finger occupies a primary position because of the interesting conclusions that can be reached from its careful examination.

The first characteristic you should look at is the junction with the rest of the hand; if it is visibly narrower in relation to the upper development of the phalanges, this indicates an element of sensuality. Then move on to identify what type the finger is.

Average length
This indicates pronounced talents and a marked personality, albeit discreetly hidden.

Long
The personality is complex, with marked analytical and introspective abilities, but with a need for lengthy reflection which inevitably leads to slow reactions.

Short
This indicates an impulsive, passionate nature and a facility for instinctive reactions.

Knotty
If the most accentuated joint is the top one (that nearest the nail), this indicates the presence of an independent spirit and a certain scepticism, while if the most accentuated joint is the lowest one it reveals a marked practical sense. But beware – if it is too accentuated the indication is less positive, as the personality in question is often blocked by suspicion and exaggerated caution to such an extent that the normal impulses are strangled. In such cases it is not uncommon to discover almost maniacal tendencies in the subject such as an obsessive sense of order.

Vertical lines
If there is only one, very marked line, this is a wise, balanced individual. If, however, the lines are short but more numerous, they indicate an open and frank character when on the first phalange, mathematical logic when on the second phalange, and the ability to concentrate and a flexible nature when on the third.

Horizontal lines
This denotes a cold, detached and often calculating character.

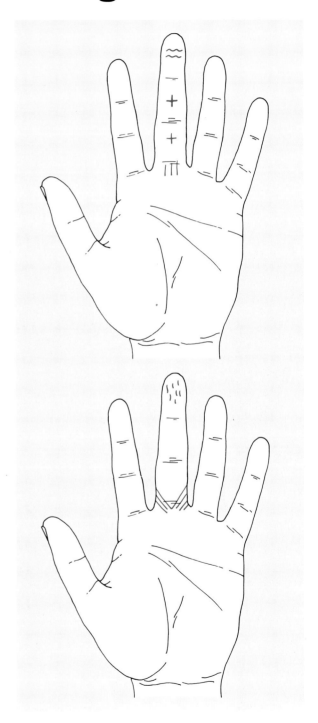

The drawing on the right shows the marks which the Chinese palmists look for when analysing the meaning of lines on the middle finger. A middle finger of average length is slightly longer than the third finger, and indicates a well-balanced attitude to daily tasks and spiritual and moral affairs. If the finger is no longer than the third finger it suggests a lack of business acumen. The subject will be unlikely to do well in business for very long because he or she makes impulsive decisions and tends to take unnecessary risks

The third finger

The ring finger is known as the digit of Apollo (or the Sun digit); it reveals the subject's aesthetic qualities and ideals. Its length is normal if it is slightly longer than the index finger, and shorter than the middle finger by about the same amount.

Long
This indicates a tendency to live in an imaginary world, to dream of success in the romantic or artistic field. It is typical of a person who is a little introverted and sensitive and who lives more in fantasy than in reality.

Excessively long
When the length is excessive (if the ring finger is as long as the middle finger) this means that the subject allows himself or herself to be carried along dangerously by his or her own instincts. A love of gambling and of risk can create economic and moral chaos.

Short
If the ring finger is shorter than the index finger it means that the person concentrates his or her energies in the material, commercial field, while at the same time regretting abandoning earlier aspirations in the artistic and aesthetic field. This characteristic is encountered in the hands of failed artists and of art dealers, antiquarians and collectors. The short ring finger is also a sign of frustration; the individual feels that he or she is not appreciated as much as he or she ought to be.

Deformed or abnormal
Medical palmistry has established that deformation or abnormality of the ring finger is frequently associated with cardiac disorders, an emotional disposition, irregular palpitations and minor malfunctions of the heart. However, these disorders are more of a nervous than of an organic nature and are cured by relaxation and sedatives.

First phalange curved towards the palm
If the phalange with the nail tends to curve towards the inside of the palm when the hand is at rest it indicates an individual who is somewhat impressionable and easily influenced, with a lively aesthetic sense.

Fleshy first phalange
This reveals a sensual and instinctive nature which is difficult to control rationally.

Long first phalange
This person tends to magnify his or her own love of beauty and seeks, albeit in a disorganized manner, to fulfil it. It can also indicate narcissism and sensuality, especially if other signs confirm this.

Short first phalange
This indicates a person whose dreams and ideals are compromised in order to achieve realistic goals. The subject does not have a very strong character, but has good sense and is adaptable.

Harmonious second phalange
If the second phalange is in perfect harmony with the other two in terms of length and well-proportioned shape, this indicates a conciliatory character always capable of finding a reasonable solution. This person still has ideals, but he or she is prepared to renounce the most utopian of them in order to comply with everyday realities.

Disharmonious second phalange
When the second phalange is out of proportion with the other two, this means the owner has a complex character and has great difficulty in attaining his or her own dreams.

Short third phalange
When the last phalange (the lowest) is very short, this reveals resignation in renouncing virtually all artistic aspirations in the interests of earning money. Some of this money, however, will be used to buy material comforts which have aesthetic appeal.

Fleshy third phalange
This denotes a love of the niceties of life. Such people are always keen to make a good impression.

The little finger

The little finger might appear to be the least important finger of the hand but it is certainly not. It is also known as the 'digit of Mercury' (the planet of the intellect) and in addition to the qualities of the mind, it reveals two particular aspects of the personality – intuition and sexual behaviour.

Average length
If the little finger is normal and does not extend beyond the base of the first phalange of the ring finger, this means that the person has a lively mentality, a good business sense and a balanced sex life.

Long
If the little finger extends beyond the base of the first phalange of the ring finger, this reveals an individual who is good at extricating himself or herself from arguments, is extremely diplomatic and rather cunning. The length of the little finger is also an indication of sexual inquisitiveness.

Short
If the little finger does not reach to the base of the first phalange of the ring finger, this denotes intelligence and a good memory. It is also, however, a sign of a poor ability to gain esteem. In the sexual field, this person suffers from inhibitions and secret fears. On the psychological plane, he or she is predisposed to nervous tension and stress.

Large and stumpy
This is a sign of a somewhat scheming character, not always loyal. It belongs, however, to lively, self-assured individuals.

Thin
This almost always reveals a state of physical weakness. It also, however, denotes sensitivity of spirit, sophisticated intelligence and an emotional nature.

Bent and distorted
This characteristic, which is often hereditary, almost always reveals a predisposition towards hypothyroidism (deficiency of the thyroid gland). This subject tends to fantasise because of an exessively lively imagination: he or she is sometimes aggressive, and suffers from a minor persecution mania. If the little finger, in addition to being distorted, is also excessively long, this reveals sexually perverted individuals who are fond of intrigue.

Set well apart from the other fingers
A little finger which tends to separate from the other fingers, especially when the hand is holding something, denotes sexual or psychological conflicts both with partners and with parents. If, in addition to separating, the little finger also moves upwards on holding something, this indicates a slightly effeminate nature in a man and a certain snobbishness in a woman.

Making a very low joint with the hand
If the point at which the little finger joins the hand is lower than that of the other fingers, the individual suffers from complexes in relation to his or her mother or father (or both) and this situation creates difficulties in relations with the opposite sex. These problems are not serious, however, and they can be overcome by growing maturity and a loving relationship.

Folded in towards the palm
This may reveal a minor kidney disorder.

A long first phalange
A very long first phalange reveals intuition and a bent for study.

Short first phalange
This shows intelligence but little willpower. Such people do not have the will to apply themselves to studying, but fortunately they have resources of imagination and are able to improvise.

Long second phalange
This reveals a lively intellect combined with talent (possibly artistic) and imagination.

Short second phalange
This person's talents are smothered by his or her shyness and timidity. He or she is heavily influenced by others.

A deep furrow on the second phalange
This often denotes sexual disorders.

Long third phalange
This subject will have a good relationship with the family and with the opposite sex. It denotes a communicative character, intuition and adaptability.

Wide and short third phalange
This betrays definite sensuality, limited powers of judgement and lack of sincerity.

A ring on the little finger
If a woman wears a ring on the little finger this reveals the most beautiful qualities of Mercury: a lively intelligence, imagination and responsiveness. It is also a sign of sexual inquisitiveness.

The thumb

The thumb is the most important part of the hand, being the symbol of the strengths that govern willpower, logic, love, vitality and strength of character. It is the digit of Venus.

The two phalanges of the thumb must be analysed separately. The upper phalange in particular tells you about the subject's willpower; the lower phalange relates primarily to the powers of reasoning.

Long
If, when held straight, the thumb extends further than half way along the index finger, this is a sign of a lively, enterprising character. If the thumb is also large and broad, it indicates vitality and, sometimes, an arrogant and violent nature.

Short
If, when held straight, the thumb does not reach halfway along the index finger, its owner has a serious and tenacious character with a marked practical sense. It is also a sign of loyalty and devotion.

Very short
This denotes a somewhat narrow mind, in some cases with little intelligence.

Straight and rigid
This belongs to individuals who are sure of themselves and inflexible in their ideas.

Flexible
This means that the owner is versatile and diplomatic. However, he or she lacks physical and moral strength and needs guidance and stimulation.

Knotty
This denotes a strong character and an imaginative personality.

Smooth
This indicates an aristocratic nature, rather lazy and indolent. It is typical of those who love comfort and luxury.

Low
If the junction between the thumb and the index finger is very low and if the thumb is a long way away from the rest of the hand, forming a right angle, this indicates an independent, liberal and humanitarian character.

Hidden
If the thumb tends to fold in towards the palm and is often concealed in the fist it reveals tension and insecurity.

Thin
This denotes a lack of vitality, especially if the thumb is also short and pointed. It also indicates moral weakness.

Backward
If, when the hand is stretched, the thumb curves backwards, it is a sign of generosity and altruism.

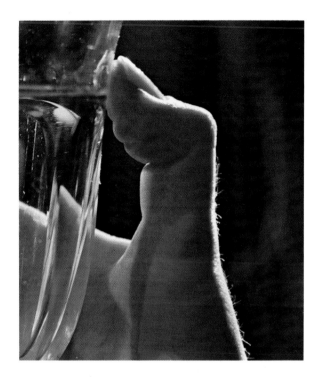

Average length
A thumb is regarded as normal when it reaches exactly midway along the index finger. It is a sign of a strong-willed, rational, tenacious and faithful character.

First phalange longer than the second
This indicates a decisive and determined character. It also reveals impatience and bossiness, however.

Average-length first phalange
This belongs to people who have no desire to dominate others but are able to stand up to anyone who seeks to dominate them.

Very broad, short first phalange
When the first phalange is club-shaped, large and bulbous, its owner is aggressive and easily angered.

Second phalange longer than the first
When the lower phalange is longer than the upper, its owner has good analytical and critical powers and cannot be dissuaded of his or her opinions. He or she will, however, lack willpower and be impractical. If this second phalange is also narrower in the middle it is a sign of a brilliant and sophisticated mind and considerable tact.

First and second phalange of equal length
These are people of uncommon intelligence, equilibrium and strength of character.

Nails and illnesses

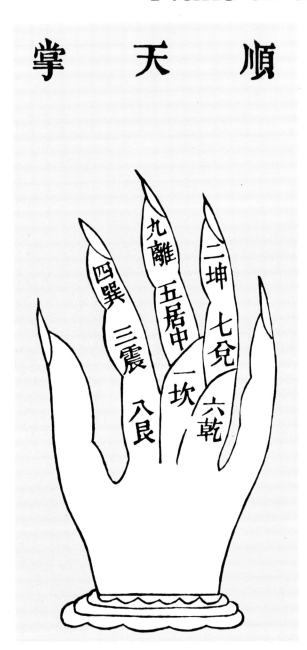

掌　天　順

九離　五居中　一坎

四巽　三震　八艮

二坤　七兑　六乾

This Drawing of the Chiromantic Hand *is from a medieval Chinese manual in the British Museum Library in London*

Palmistry is used not only to identify particular aspects of the character but also to obtain information on the general state of health.

The art of 'reading' the presages or after-effects of illnesses in the fingernails has been known in the West for many centuries: the famous Medical School in Salerno, Italy, held this discipline in great regard. In the Orient, and in Tibet in particular, people were convinced that careful observation of the nails could help to prevent illness.

The shape, colour and blemishes of the fingernails, for those who know how to read them, are valuable sources of information on certain glandular, cardiac, vascular and intestinal malfunctions.

Almond-shaped
This indicates good mental and physical equilibrium, especially if they are naturally polished and have little moons at the base.

Fragile
This points to a calcium and vitamin deficiency. If the fingernails also have no moons and are thin and broken, they indicate glandular deficiencies and strong, barely-suppressed emotions.

Claw-like
These accompany a robust physique. In the case of very hard nails that bend forwards, they also indicate ferocious jealousy and possessiveness.

Short and wide
This reveals a tendency to develop high blood pressure. After middle age, it can also signify cardiac disorders. The owners are intelligent individuals who can discuss anything but who always want to argue for the pleasure of being perverse.

Short and narrow
These are typical of individuals of a somewhat delicate constitution. They are shy, introverted and hypersensitive.

Long and narrow
Such nails indicate psychological problems as a result of hypersensitivity and phobias.

Ridged
Ridged nails are a symptom of intestinal disorders which can turn to colitis or gastritis. If they appear at an advanced age, they can be a precursor of rheumatism or arthritis.

Convex
If the convexity is moderate it means good health. If it is accentuated and associated with highly developed finger-tips, malfunctions of the liver, the respiratory tract and the cardiovascular system are to be suspected.

Concave
If the nails are flattened in the centre, they reveal malnu-

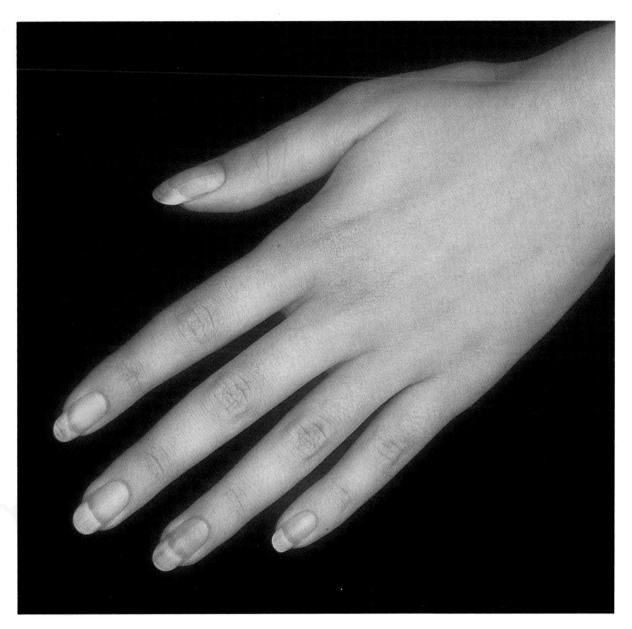

trition. If the concavity is spoon-shaped, this is indicative of glandular malfunction.

Large moons
If the moons are too large this indicates hyperthyroidism, or an over active thyroid gland.

No moons
This denotes a physique with good reserves of strength and a pleasant and communicative character.

Blemishes or white spots
These indicate anxiety and a slight mineral deficiency.

Bitten
Those who bite their nails, especially as adults, betray an unstable character, a sense of guilt and recurrent sexual problems.

Nail totally absent
This is a sign of congenital or hereditary disorders. The same applies to nails that have been split since birth and continue to grow with the same defect.

Pale
This indicates anaemia.

6

Chinese Palmistry

The civilization of China is thousands of years old and the Chinese probably developed palmistry as a science long before it was recognized in the West. Some of the emphases are different from those of Western palmistry – the wrist, for example, is considered to be particularly significant, as are ephemeral marks. Because these marks may appear and disappear within a short space of time, the skill of the Oriental palmist lies in catching them as well as interpreting them.

Different meanings are attributed to certain ephemeral marks according to when they appear, how long for, and the clarity and depth of the line. The mark of the word 'woman', for instance, is a positive sign of good fortune, accentuated if it is crossed by a line. If the line is deep, however, the good fortune is negated. The simultaneous appearance of two or more of the marks imbues them with yet another meaning.

Chinese palmistry is extremely complex and a great deal of learning and experience is required to interpret the hand correctly according to its precepts. This chapter simply provides some guidelines to just a few of the fundamental principles which may stimulate you to further reading on this fascinating art.

The Chinese wrist

In Chinese palmistry, the study of the wrist is particularly important. The wrist is regarded as the symbol of the deepest workings of the unconscious mind and it is studied down to the tiniest detail. A strong and robust wrist, for example, is a sign of great vitality, dynamism and sensuality. A thin wrist, on the other hand, denotes delicate health, spirituality and a generous spirit.

As regards the lines, the Chinese immediately look for the 'magic triple bracelet' on the wrist – i.e. three parallel horizontal lines under the palm. If they are present the subject has intellectual and moral qualities that will assure him or her of a serene and comfortable life of good fortune. A great deal of significance is attached to the 'line of jade', a bracelet that encircles the wrist completely; this sign indicates an ability to fascinate the opposite sex.

If the bracelets are irregular or broken, this means that difficulties will arise, although these can be overcome. If there is a cross at the centre of the 'magic triple bracelet', this means that exceptional physical strength is accompanied by an exceptional power to seduce. If the lines of the bracelet are chained you can expect a series of positive events linked together in sequence, especially in the fields of work and earnings. If the lines of the wrist are directed towards the palm, specifically towards the base of the little finger, this means that the need for change and adventure will take the subject on extensive travels.

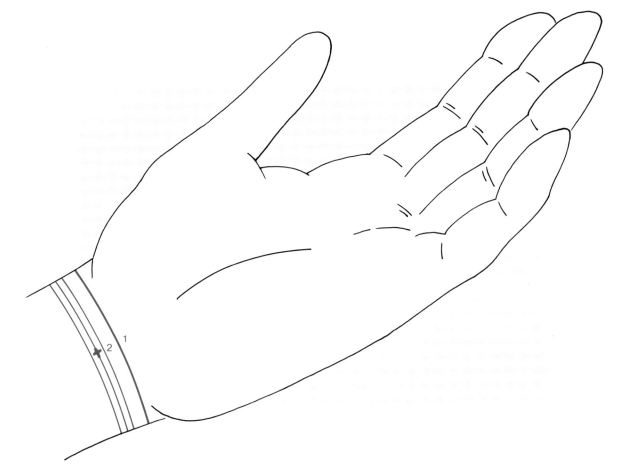

1. Wrist line directed towards the base of the little finger

2. The 'magic triple bracelet' with a cross in the centre

Ephemeral marks

Many marks appear on the hands, sometimes for only very brief periods. Chinese palmistry, and Oriental palmistry in general, attributes great importance to these marks, although they are not easy to interpret. Western palmistry pays less attention to them but there are certain marks which it is useful to know. The future is not fixed and while we exist we influence, and are influenced by, our environment. The limits that are imposed upon a person tend to be characteristics he or she has inherited from his or her ancestors. Otherwise, to a certain extent at least, man is master of his own fate, and any changes in attitude or influence will be reflected in the changes which occur in the hand. Bear in mind when looking for the Chinese ephemeral marks that the value of them depends upon the clarity and depth of the line and the period of time for which it appears. Consequently, correct interpretation requires a great deal of experience and you should regard the following definitions as guidelines only.

Flying needles

Flying needles are short parallel-lines (not usually particularly numerous) identified by their intense red colour. According to Chinese palmistry, they announce success. But beware; if they are crossed by another line, the flying needles have an unhappy meaning – they presage a serious problem.

The roof

The roof, also known as the sign of the two branches in Chinese palmistry, is not an auspicious sign when the angle is acute. Its appearance is less unfavourable when the angle is more obtuse. It indicates temporary problems.

Bangles

Bangles are two small adjacent circles. They always have a positive meaning: if they are red, they announce material and emotional riches.

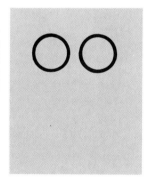

The devil

The devil is an unfavourable sign. It indicates inability to decide, cowardice and a deceitful disposition. Since it is not an easy sign to identify, it should be examined carefully. Remember that it appears only from time to time and is temporary.

The sign of the hooked fish

This too is a favourable sign. It indicates power and personal satisfaction.

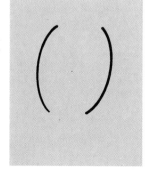

Lascivious desires

Lascivious desires are thin, close lines which are commonly found on the Mount of Venus. They indicate sexual love. If they appear on the upper part of the Mount of Venus they indicate an ability for sexual relationships even at an advanced age.

The chequerboard

When this appears on the Mount of Venus it indicates depression and a reduced ability to cope with difficulties. When it appears elsewhere on the palm of the hand it forecasts changes for the better and the possibility of resolving even the most difficult problems.

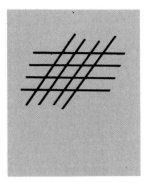

The double boat

The double boat is a figure of eight. It is an unfavourable mark, auguring problems and unpleasant surprises. It applies only when well defined and when there are no breaks in the lines making up the figure.

The staircase of jade

This is always a harbinger of good tidings. In particular, it foretells success in academic examinations and the prospect of high social standing.

The double well

The double well is complex and easy to confuse with other marks. Chinese palmistry attributes a favourable meaning to it, regarding it as a presage of material and moral satisfaction.

The star of the south

The star of the south is made up of an even number of small circles or cavities. If it is red and shows up on a smooth palm, it indicates riches. If, however, it is pale and is crossed by a line, or if it appears on two phalanges of the middle finger, it has an unfavourable meaning.

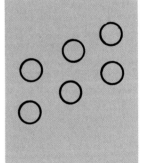

The ladder of jade

This denotes wisdom and intelligence. When repeated, it announces good fortune and success in business.

The extension

The extension is always a favourable sign; it announces success. It also means the extinction of old desires that have never been satisfied.

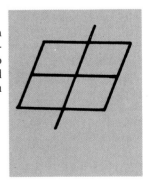

Braid

Braid announces high positions and honours. It is of particular significance for those following a military career.

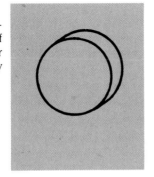

The word 'woman'

This is the sign of sensuality. Depending on its position on the hand, it means: support from others; a happy family situation (because of a woman); prosperity; a good social position. When the sign is crossed by a line its positive meanings are attenuated, becoming negative if the line is deep.

The lotus

This ephemeral mark must consist of two converging lines which do not actually join. When clearly defined, it indicates mysticism and a tendency to withdraw from reality. Overall, it is a favourable sign.

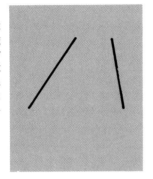

The word 'nail'

This is an unfavourable sign. The nail represents an obstacle which it will be difficult to overcome. However, it is possible also to read this sign as a 'key': this means the presence of an obstacle which it would be better to try to get around rather than tackle head on.

The crescent moon

This is a favourable mark presaging good fortune in business and success in love. Beware, however, that it is not crossed by a line: in this case it is an unfavourable sign, particularly with regard to work.

The word 'ten'

This is a relatively common sign. In Western palmistry it has a negative meaning: in Oriental palmistry it is interpreted in each individual case, and is not necessarily inauspicious. The Chinese regard it as sign of success and of a serene life, and at times even of good fortune and unexpected assistance.

The string of coins

This indicates economic success and high status. Those who are striving for social position should regard this sign as extremely auspicious.

The word 'then'

This is a negative sign that indicates difficulties and inability to achieve long-term aims.

The word 'fire'

Its appearance should put you on guard against anything that might be symbolized by fire, such as anger, exaltation, over-hasty decisions. This too is an ambivalent mark that can be read in different ways.

The eye of the elephant

This is a favourable sign that appears infrequently. It indicates loyalty, fairness and honesty.

The word 'hand'

This is an auspicious sign, indicating purity of feeling and loyalty. It is not always easy to identify and in particular it should not be confused with the next sign.

The sign of the fish

An auspicious omen of a serene life. When it crosses a digit of the hand like the tail of a fish, it announces money. When it appears on two fingers it means money and honours.

The word 'earth'

This indicates a cold heart and disloyal behaviour in the interests of personal gain.

The field

The field, which is quite characteristic and unmistakeable, is a happy sign. It infallibly augurs success in business and good fortune. The more polished and deep its component lines, the stronger the message of happiness.

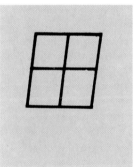

The word 'valley'

This is a highly favourable sign. Its appearance indicates long life, success at work, good relations with others and good fortune.

The precious spiral

This is not a common sign. Its appearance indicates achievement at work and in social life. When it remains on the hand for some time, personal satisfaction and honours are to be expected as well as financial gain.

Wells of gold

This is a difficult sign to find, inasmuch as it can be easily confused with others of a similar nature. Always favourable, it indicates success in business, especially in the case of the purchase or sale of land or property.

The sign of the tortoise

This too is a relatively favourable sign. It announces the attainment of fame and great honours. Given its complexity, it is difficult to identify it accurately. It should not be confused with signs of similar appearance.

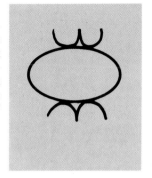

The large wheel

This is an ambivalent sign. When it appears on the mounts it is favourable but when on the lines it is inauspicous. On the thumb it indicates a lively intelligence: elsewhere it may signify mysticism.

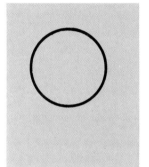

The sign of the triangle

This is another ambivalent sign that can signify success but also difficulty and bad behaviour.

The seal of the flower

This is an omen of social achievement and gain. For students it augurs success in examinations.

The sign of three cats

This is always a favourable sign, indicating success in undertakings nearest to your heart. It also signifies a long life and good fortune in love.

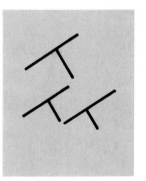

The sign of six flowers

This is one of the most favourable ephemeral marks (and one of the most uncommon). It signifies success in everything: in love, in business, in social life. It augurs wellbeing and prestige even at an advanced age.

The flight of the geese

This too is always a favourable sign, indicating success and prestige. It should be composed of five lines which do not touch.

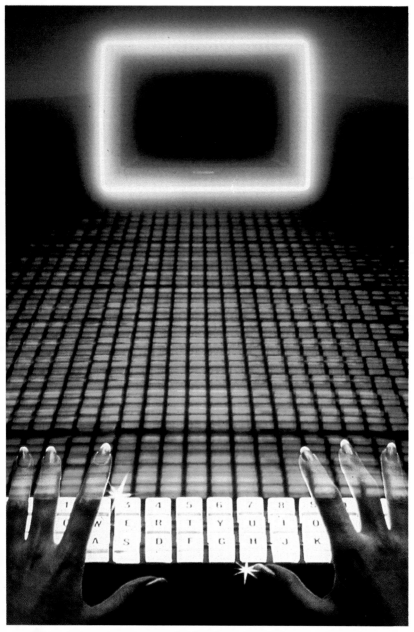

7

Questions and Answers

By now you have mastered the main elements of palmistry and will, no doubt, be anxious to tackle your first subject (you will almost certainly have read your own palm already!). Palmistry is such a complex science that covering all its points would require an encyclopedia in several volumes. However, as you read an increasing number of palms you will discover there are certain questions that are often posed by your subjects – partly because there are some features that are common to a large number of hands and partly because the human preoccupations of love, sex, children, power and money are universal!

Consequently, this chapter tackles a number of questions that are likely to arise: for example, the meaning of a short heart line; the significance of the thumb curving towards the index finger; whether cold hands really do indicate a cold heart; if the absence of a fate line means there are no predetermined future events; and how a jealous nature is delineated. Together with the information you have gained from the previous chapters, this section completes a thorough grounding in the fascinating science of palmistry on which you can build as your experience in hand analysis grows.

A short heart line

'My heart line stops just over halfway across my palm, at the level of the middle finger. Does this mean that I shall have short-lived love affairs?'

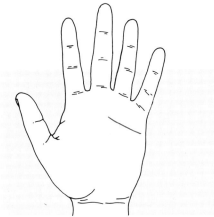

The length of the heart line relates not so much to the length of love affairs as to your ability to love. A short heart line indicates a tendency to avoid becoming too involved in relationships. Termination under the middle finger (the Mount of Saturn) emphasizes a more sensual than affectionate nature. It should, however, be remembered that the lines can change. People who in time feel a growing need to love with generosity and in depth will see their heart line lengthen until it reaches the base of the index finger.

A thumb which bends towards the index finger

'My hand is quite attractive, even though I say so myself. But my thumb, instead of curving outwards, bends towards the index finger. Is it true that this is a sign of childishness?'

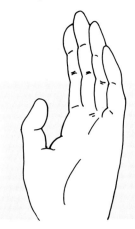

The thumb is the most important digit in the hand – the only one that has vast potential for movement. It represents vitality, willpower and self-expression. A thumb inclined outwards as normal indicates a desire on the part of the owner to express his or her own personality and to communicate with others. If, however, it curves inwards it denotes unsociability and also a touch of avarice. It would only be a sign of childishness if totally hidden inside the hand. This is seen in people who have remained mentally childish and who, although adults, continue to automatically cover the thumb with the other digits of the hand as do very young babies.

The sign of an artistic temperament

'I have heard it said that long, pointed fingers are a sign of an artistic temperament. Is that so?'

One of the twentieth century's greatest painters, Pablo Picasso

Long fingers indicate a strong tendency towards analysis, reflection and detail more than an artistic temperament. If exaggeratedly long they reveal a certain craving to perform which is characteristic of artists, but it is regarded here more as a negative than a positive trait.

Having pointed fingers, however, is unquestionably a sign of aesthetic taste and an artistic bent. They are seen in many musicians, painters and designers. An interesting test is to open the hand suddenly, and as naturally as possible: if the middle finger is closer to the ring finger, you can be certain that you are a born artist. If the middle finger is closer to the index finger, however, this means that exhibitionism is the prevailing trait in your character!

Do breaks in lines represent illnesses?

'I have a life line that is broken by numerous small transverse lines. I have been told that each of these relates to an illness. Is this so?'

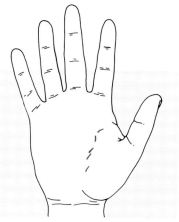

No, fortunately it isn't. The transverse lines are merely an indication of a danger that you can avoid by taking particular care of your health and which you must in any case compare with other signs. First, each of the small lines must appear on both hands. Second, bear in mind that if one appears on the left hand and not on the right, this means that it is a hereditary weakness, or represents a poor state of health from which one of your parents (or both) was suffering at the time of your conception. In this case the risk of illness is minimal, if not zero.

Check whether the break in the life line is flanked by parallel lines. If it is the risk is a good deal less serious, as this second line indicates your energy reserves which, in the event of illness or injury, will come to your assistance. The small transverse lines must be long and deep in order to indicate any worrying illness; otherwise they signify only a temporary drop in vitality or minor illnesses.

What does the side of the hand reveal?

'I have examined the edge of my hand carefully and have noticed many horizontal lines below my little finger, just above the wrist. What is the meaning of these lines? I should also like to know whether it is true that a person with a very fleshy or soft edge such as I have has an ability to accumulate riches.'

The side of the hand (by the little finger), called the 'percussion', is examined in profile, bearing in mind that the upper part relates to fertility and sentimental bonds, the middle part to the physical life and the lower part to the imagination. Many small horizontal lines in the lower part indicate a rich imagination that leads the subject to daydream of escape, travel and exciting changes. The fact that your percussion is very fleshy and soft does not mean an ability to accumulate riches but undoubtedly signifies a realistic approach to life. Coupled with your vivid imagination and enterprising spirit, this means you have the ability to recognise what will bring you material benefit and you are not afraid to go far afield to attain it.

A mount between two fingers

'I should like some information on the Mount of Jupiter. I know that it should be located under the index finger and that if it is well developed it signifies an ability to make one's mark in life. My Mount of Jupiter, however, is in a strange position – half under the index finger and half under the middle finger. What does this mean?'

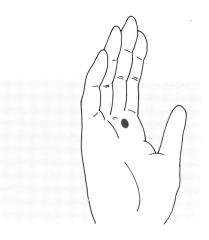

It is not unusual to find cases in which a mount extends to a greater or lesser degree under the adjacent finger. This does not reduce the positive significance of the mount in question – in fact, it has the advantage of also acquiring in part the characteristics associated with the other finger. In the case in point, a well-developed Mount of Jupiter under the index finger reveals an ambitious and active temperament but also one which is quite conservative. This kind of mount indicates that the owner will move steadily and directly towards achieving a good living or will manage to make his or her mark in life. In addition, by also occupying part of the base of the middle finger, it shares the qualities of Saturn – decisiveness and firmness. The combination of all these qualities may well lead to success.

The hand of a driver

'On observing my hands I have noticed a definite change in the lines on the right hand. They have become closer and deeper, while those on the left hand have remained as they always were. Is this normal?'

Ex-Formula One racing driver Keke Rosberg has drivers' hands

It is totally normal if, for example, you spend many hours per day at the wheel of a car and you are, like most people, right-handed. It is also normal if you don't drive a car but do a manual job that requires you to use the right hand frequently. Many of the marks on the palms of our hands are 'occupational', indicating the job that we do rather than our fate or our character. The same is true of the colour of our hands, their hardness, and very often also their shape. Just as the driver has well-defined hands so a typist has characteristic fingers and lines, as do the boxer, the farm-worker and the writer.

Which hand should you read?

'Some people say that it is better to examine the palm of the left hand, while others say that it should be the right. Which is correct?'

There is no precise rule, although palmists normally prefer to start by reading the left hand, since this one tends to retain its original, natural state better. Being the hand that is least used in daily activities, it has not been subject to the same wear and tear as the right one; in addition, it tends to show the small alterations made to the lines by the subject's development over the course of the years. It is easier to see the deepening of a groove, the elongation of a line or the greater protrusion of a mount due to a change of character. After examining the left hand, however, it is necessary to look at the right to check whether all the lines are the same. In fact, all conclusions are of value only if the lines are confirmed in both hands.

An even better system is to observe both hands superficially before moving on to a more detailed examination to check whether they are similar. It is worth feeling their consistency, on the backs and on the palms, noting whether one is softer, paler or colder than the other. Finally, look for a difference in size (although this may only be slight and relatively difficult to identify). Any of these differences reveal contradictions in the personality from the outset and emphasize the importance of taking account only of those lines and marks that are present on both hands.

What does the shape of the nails reveal?

'I should like to know whether there is any relationship between fragility of the fingernails and weak health. Also, what is the meaning of fingernails that bend forward like claws?'

Fragile fingernails indicate that the owner's state of health is less than perfect. There may be a vitamin and calcium deficiency. If the nails are ridged the owner is lacking in energy and liable to suffer exhaustion or chronic illness. Nails that are bent forwards are a sign of vitality – but also of a possessive and passionate nature!

Do dots on the heart line relate to love affairs?

'Looking carefully at my hand, I have found three red dots on the heart line. Does this relate to the number of love affairs I shall have?'

Elizabeth Taylor, famed for her beauty and her numerous marriages

These red dots do not indicate the number of love affairs but the number of heartbreaks. They mean that three times in your life you will suffer as someone slips away from you or in some other way does not allow you an easy relationship. Take a good look at the location of the three red dots to establish both the time and the type of love in question. If the reddish speck is at the level of the ring finger (dominated by Apollo), the heartbreak will relate to your youth and is the result of an infatuation.

If it is at the level of the middle finger (dominated by Saturn) this indicates an extremely complicated love affair experienced at around the age of 40. If the reddish speck is at the end of the heart line (at the level of the index finger, dominated by Jupiter) this means that you will fall for someone at a mature age who is not available to you, bringing consequent anxieties and tensions.

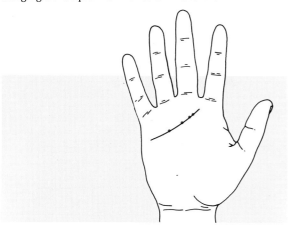

Short fingers and a large hand

'I have become aware that I have very short fingers in relation to the palm of my hand, while my husband has very large hands out of proportion with his height and build (which are average).'

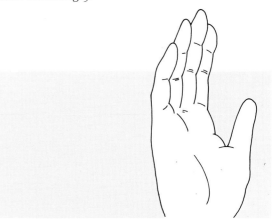

Short fingers indicate typically feminine characteristics such as intuition, impulsiveness and demonstrativeness. They are also associated with intellectual qualities such as intense concentration and the ability to assimilate new concepts very quickly. In addition, they reveal a sense of realism and considerable dynamism. You should therefore be pleased with your fingers!

Your husband's large hand is typical of a person who has difficulty in condensing a large number of thoughts into a single concept. He is a man who needs to reflect at length on things and to examine every detail. This too can be regarded as a good quality, particularly if your husband devotes himself to academic research. He has another merit, too: he won't allow himself to be easily influenced.

A hairy hand

'My husband has very hairy hands. Does this give any indication of a person's character?'

The degree of hairiness of the hand can provide certain indications of vitality and sexuality. If the hairs are sparse and in little tufts here and there on the back of the hand, this means that the subject allows himself to be carried away by his sexual impulses.

Numerous and dense hairs indicate a man of considerable physical strength who can be brusque and aggressive. A complete absence of hairs on a man's hand can mean physical weakness or extremely delicate health.

If there are a number of hairs on the back of a woman's hands this suggests a hormonal imbalance.

What does a fleshy thumb signify?

'Is it true that a hand with a fleshy thumb and a relatively long third phalange of the index finger is the sign of notable strength of character? I have also read that it could be a sign of thoughtfulness.'

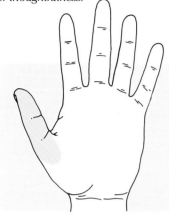

This type of hand unquestionably suggests that the qualities of idealism, strength of thought and intellectual lucidity prevail over the impulsive side of the character. These are signs that recall the features of the 'philosophic hand' of those who are engaged in intellectual activities. If the fingers are also flexible, this is a nonconformist individual who is capable of intense concentration.

What are the signs of jealousy?

'I have heard that it is possible to determine whether or not a person has a jealous nature by reading their hands . . .'

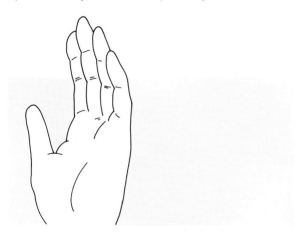

It is quite possible to identify whether a person is jealous by nature from the lines and features of the hand – the term 'jealousy' being used to mean over-possessiveness, suspicion and little trust in the person loved. A jealous individual also shows little trust of himself or herself, and the first sign that reveals this is an initial joining, over a long section, of the head and life lines. This indicates shyness and a low level of self-confidence. Another characteristic of jealousy is an excessively long heart line, disappearing at the joint between the index and middle finger. The fingers will be knotty rather than smooth and the little finger tends to be short. The thumb, on the other hand, is excessively large. The back of the hand may be lined.

Signs of a passionate temperament

'A palmist, looking at my hand, told me that the signs of my passionate temperament were very clear. I didn't ask what they were at the time, but I should like to know now. In general, what are the characteristics shown in the hand of a passionate person?'

Clark Gable and Vivien Leigh in Gone With The Wind *in 1939*

There are many signs that indicate a passionate temperament: first, a well-developed and reddened Mount of Venus (the broad, fleshy bump under the thumb). If this mount has intersecting lines in a grid formation it means that the owner tends to give way to instinctive sensuality. Another important sign is a chained heart line; this too reveals the existence of strong sexual desires.

There is also a particular feature that you should look for – the ring of Venus. It is a small semi-circle which is sometimes present between the ring finger and the middle finger. Having this ring at all is evidence of a very sensual nature: if the ring is broken in one or more places, it means that the owner's sexual impulses are sometimes uncheckable.

means that mental activity in excessive and is liable to suffocate the natural impulses. If the prominences of the middle zone are excessive, this means that the subject's interests will be centred on work and success and everything else will be disregarded. If the lower part predominates, this betrays a person who seeks only to obtain money, by whatever means, and to satisfy his or her erotic desires.

What are the three parts of the palm?

'A palmist told me that as soon as he was shown the palm of a hand, the first thing he did was to look at its three parts. I should like to know exactly what these three parts are and what they represent in terms of the character and fate?'

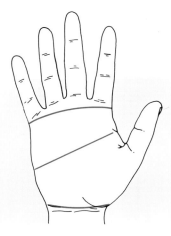

Sub-division of the hand into three parts relates to a principle that was also adopted by physiognomists. They divided the face into the upper part (the forehead), the middle part (the nose), and the lower part (the chin). In palmistry, the palm of the hand is divided into an upper part, which extends from the tip of the finger to its base; a middle part, which extends from the base of the finger to an imaginary line that crosses the hand horizontally, starting from the internal curve of the thumb; and a lower part that runs from this imaginary horizontal line to the wrist.

The upper part reflects the mental or spiritual world; the middle part is associated with the practical sphere of daily activities; the lower part corresponds to the material and sexual life. If these three parts are in harmony you can assume a good mental and physical balance is present. In order to reach this initial judgement you must bear in mind that the upper part (the fingers) must be as long as the rest of the palm (more or less) and that the prominences of the other two parts must each occupy only their own zone. If the fingers are very much longer than the palm, this

The marks of ambition

'Are there any marks or lines on the hand that indicate an ambitious, social-climbing nature?'

Joan Collins, an actress frequently typecast as very ambitious

There is no single mark that indicates ambition or a thirst for success. Begin by checking the Mount of Jupiter (the fleshy prominence under the index finger) to see if it is very obvious. Then carefully examine the index finger itself. If this is short and spatulate it reveals extremely strong ambition which will be manifested by a certain amount of arrogance. If the index finger is long, this means that the ambition is controlled and patient. If it is extremely long, it denotes unbridled ambition. It is also interesting to note the thumb. In a social climber it is solid, strong and at the same time very soft.

Irish writer Oscar Wilde served a prison sentence for homosexuality

Effeminacy

'There are some men who have hands that are quite unmasculine – very slender and without a trace of hair. What does this mean? Are they effeminate?'

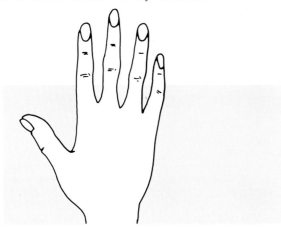

The physical characteristics of effeminacy cannot be based solely on the shape and type of hand – a youthful,

hairless face, long eyelashes, a soft mouth and so on will also be present.

It may be said that if the hand is exceptionally smooth and light in a man, it reveals a romantic, dreaming nature. This is the hand of a musician, a poet, a mystic or of a person who lives in a world far removed from day-to-day reality and tends to shut himself or herself up in his or her own world of fantasy.

But beware: sometimes hands such as these accompany an astute or rascally individual who is a master of skilful deceit. These are the magicians, the conjurers, the cardsharps, the pickpockets and a whole range of adventurers who seek easy gains.

Is a crooked little finger hereditary?

'The last phalange of the little finger of my right hand is very crooked. My mother has the same characteristic. Is it possible that my children will also be born with a crooked little finger?'

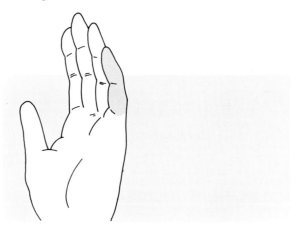

It is not only possible but probable. A crooked little finger (particularly on the right hand) is a relatively widespread hereditary characteristic, for which there is no specific explanation.

Is the saying 'Cold hands, warm heart', true?

'Palmistry also includes an assessment of the warmth or coldness of the hand. Is the saying "Cold hands, warm heart" really true?'

In the popular view, 'Cold hands, warm heart' means that the colder a person's hands, the warmer the character. In reality, this is not true: it can in fact be said that a cold hand indicates a tendency on the part of the person to repress his or her impulses. This is a person who, because of disappointments suffered or because of social unease, hides what he or she is feeling and finds it difficult to express affection in public.

People who always have warm hands, however, tend to communicate well with those around them and to express their love, sometimes over-dramatically. There are many cases of shy people whose hands were cold in adolescence but who, in their thirties, following happy experiences in love or marriage, have permanently warm hands.

The length of the little finger

'I have an unusual little finger. It is very long, extending almost to the same length as the index finger. The middle finger, too, has a strange feature: it is extremely flexible, and I can bend it back almost at a right angle.'

The little finger is the digit of Mercury and therefore indicates qualities of intelligence, sociability and intuition. A little finger as long as yours means that these qualities are present to a very pronounced degree. A middle finger that is so flexible reveals an adaptable, happy person, capable of getting along with anybody.

A palm dotted with small triangles

'I should like to know the meaning of a palm that is dotted with small triangles and has a well-defined head line. I often suffer from depression: is this anything to do with the features that I have outlined?'

It is in fact strange for depression to be a distinctive feature of someone who has a hand of this type. In general, a well-defined head line denotes a mind that is always able to see

the various aspects of reality clearly and with their true meaning: the owner almost verges on cynicism. A logical and rational intellect has no room for periods of depression, other than very infrequently. However, the depression would be shown by a cold and dry hand, possibly also with an excessive Mount of the Moon.

Marilyn Monroe, here with Cary Grant, committed suicide in 1962

The meaning of a short hand

'I don't quite understand the relationship between the length of the fingers and the length of the palm. It is true that a squat hand always and only indicates a violent nature?'

Heinrich Heine, nineteenth-century German Romantic poet

It is always dangerous to make generalizations as there are numerous types of hand and these should be examined in each individual considering every one of their features. However, it can be said that the three basic types are the slender hand, in which the fingers are longer than the palm; the balanced hand, in which the fingers are the same length as the palm; and the squat hand, in which the fingers are shorter than the palm.

The slender hand belongs to dreamers, artists, mystics – those who aspire towards ideals of beauty, faith, poetry or perfection.

The balanced hand generally belongs to people with a rational mentality who have a strong grasp of reality and seek the practical aspect of every undertaking. It is also a sign of good psycho-physical balance among those such as research workers, academics, mathematicians, physicians and philosophers.

The short hand belongs to materialists who seek only economic wellbeing in life, and who are prepared even to be violent to get it. They have a strong sex drive which they often exhibit aggressively. However, this hand is also shared by generous individuals who struggle courageously against social injustices or who make major sacrifices in order to bring about the fulfilment of their ideals.

In the nineteenth century, the slender hands of the romantics, artists and idealists were predominant. In the Middle Ages, the short, rough hands of the soldiers and peasants prevailed. Today it is the balanced hand, oriented towards a practical view of life, which is most common.

How many children will I have?

'Just under the little finger, on the edge of the hand, I have four small lines. Does this mean that I shall have four children?'

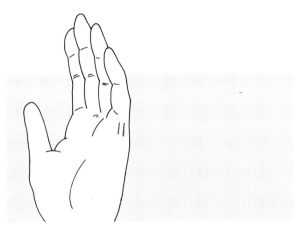

You do not say whether these are horizontal or vertical lines. The 'lines of children' are the vertical lines to be found on the edge of the hand (on the percussion). However, these lines do not indicate the exact number of children, but the owner's level of fertility. They also have a psychological meaning: they denote the degree of love of children, and the depth of paternal or maternal feeling. In assessing this, you need also to observe whether the edge of the hand is developed to a greater or lesser extent.

If the small lines visible on the edge of the hand are

horizontal, the meaning is quite different. These indicate romantic involvements. Whether these are marriages, relationships of living together or temporary but intense relationships, the lines reveal those bonds that leave an indelible mark on people's lives. The length of each line is in proportion to the intensity, rather than the duration, of the relationship: a short, deep line indicates the depth of passion. A chained line of union can, in a married person, indicate a tendency towards adultery, especially if the line is reddish in colour.

The Betrothal of Arnolfini *by the Flemish painter Jan van Eyck*

Soft and hard hands

'When I shake a person's hand, I often see them make a little grimace of pain. They say that I hurt them, that my hand is too hard. It seems to me to be a sign of great virility. Isn't a soft hand a sign of a weak character and effeminate nature?'

Cecil B. De Mille, the dynamic and dedicated American director

A hard hand essentially indicates a resolute, dynamic, positive and practical character. It is not necessarily associated with virility and can also be found in women. Excessive hardness indicates only a lack of delicacy.

Nor is it true that a hard hand is only found in people who engage in manual labour (as many believe). There are artists who have a rigid, hard hand and who pour this sign of aggressiveness and decisiveness into their work. When a hard hand also has callouses this does not always denote heavy manual work either – there are some totally lazy people who have callouses on their hands! The callous is a sign of hardness of temperament.

A soft hand does, it is true, indicate a certain weakness or apathy, especially if the hand remains virtually inert when outstretched, leaving it up to the other person to do the shaking. However, if the soft hand is also flexible and expressive this sometimes indicates an intuitive, sensitive and brilliant personality.

A balance is found between the hard hand and the soft hand in a third type of hand – the firm hand. Without being too hard, it gives an indication of energy, stability and inner confidence. This is a hand that reveals intelligence and an ability to combine theory with practice. The firm hand does not harden easily, even when its owner does manual work, while a very hard hand becomes even harder as the years go by.

Life line and line of fortune are joined

'My life line seems to me to be rather worrying: it is broken at one point and only continues a little further along. In the missing section, it is replaced by the line of fortune, which then follows alongside it for a few centimetres more, towards the wrist.'

There is no need to be alarmed when the life line is interrupted, flanked or in part replaced by the line of fortune. It does not mean that you are threatened by any illness or accident but that your existence at that stage of your life is guided more by fortuitous events than by your own will. The luckiest period of your life is that in which the line of fortune touches the life line.

Do horizontal lines on the wrist indicate a long life?

'On the edge of my wrist I have three well-defined horizontal lines. Does this mean, as I believe, that I shall live for a very long time?'

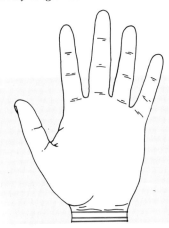

The horizontal lines found at the point at which the hand joins the wrist are known as the bracelets of long life because, if well-defined, they indicate considerable vitality and good health and, consequently, are a good omen for a long life. This characteristic must, however, also be confirmed by a good life line, long and marked.

If there are three well-defined parallel lines on the wrist, as in your case, this is the 'magic bracelet' that indicates not only a long life but also considerable physical strength and the ability to adapt physically and mentally to all circumstances. Certain works on palmistry assign 25 years of life to each line in the bracelet, and indeed four or more bracelets have been found on the wrists of many centegenarians.

American baseball ace Joe di Maggio played for the New York Yankees

Is it true there is a major line known as the ape line?

'I have heard that as well as the three lines of life, head and heart there is a fourth major line – the primitive, or ape, line. Could you provide any information on this?'

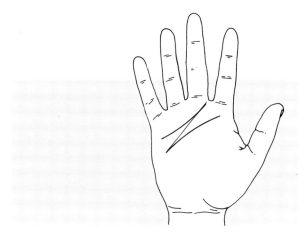

The precise name is the primitive, or ape, mark. This is not a fourth line in addition to the three basic lines of life, head and heart but a relatively rare line which in some cases joins the head and heart lines. According to a number of scholars, this single line crossing the palm of the hand could be found in primitive man and is still present in the hands of apes (hence its name).

For a time it was thought that its meaning was negative, associated with aggressive people, psychopaths or criminals. It was then found that this assessment did not apply if the hand did not contain any other abnormal features such as, for example, a deformed thumb. It was discovered, on the basis of examination of the hands of thousands of people, that this strange mark was found more frequently in the hands of aesthetes and artists, people who believed wholeheartedly in religious or aesthetic ideas, possibly to the extent of becoming fanatics.

Is a flat Mount of Venus a sign of frigidity?

'I know that the Mount of Venus relates to the individual's amorous and sexual powers. Where exactly is this mount? If it is flat or barely noticeable, does this really indicate a frigid character?'

The Mount of Venus is the fleshy protrusion under the thumb which extends almost to the wrist. There are many factors that have to be taken into account to establish the subject's level of sensuality. The mount should be not only large and well-defined but also compact and soft. If it is too prominent, coarse and hard, this means that there is a danger of brutality.

If it is relatively unpronounced and flat, this generally indicates a low level of passion and a certain aridity of the

heart. This is not always accompanied by frigidity, however. This characteristic is very often found in intellectuals who experience eroticism more in their brain than with their heart and are excited by passions that are more imaginary than real. Sometimes a small Mount of Venus is also a sign of poor physical vitality. If, however, it accompanies a very long thumb, this lack of energy is counteracted by a strong will.

A double fate line

'I have read in a number of books on palmistry that the line of fate is extremely important but that not everyone has the good fortune to have one. However, some people have two lines of fate, one parallel to the other. Is this a sign of double good fortune?'

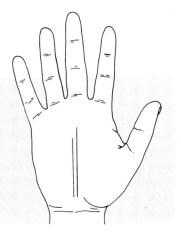

The line of fate, which generally starts at the base of the palm and runs to below the middle finger, indicates everything relating to the future density of the subject: success or failure, wealth or poverty, good fortune or ill.

In itself, therefore, the line of fate is neither favourable nor unfavourable. A great deal depends on whether it is straight, unbroken, of a good colour and well-defined. If it is all these things it indicates possibilities of achievement, happiness and good fortune. If the line is twisted, broken, too fine or pale, the omens are less good. If it starts further down the wrist and is exaggeratedly long, ending in the third phalange of the middle finger, its significance changes again and it means that much effort will be made by this person to find success but the results of his or her struggle will be largely unfruitful.

So having two lines of fate on the palm of the hand does not mean double good fortune – simply a double density. These people, while following their vocation, are attracted by another calling which is frequently contradictory and they struggle continuously to bring harmony into their life.

A red, black or blue spot

'My life line is marked by a number of red spots. One of my acquaintances has blue spots, and another has black. I should like to know the meaning of these coloured spots.'

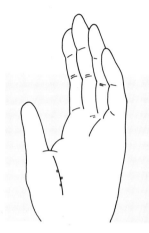

A red, blue or black spot on the life line can indicate the possibility of minor health disorders. However, this diagnosis would have to be confirmed by similar spots on the other hand and also on the heart line.

In general terms, it can be said that a red spot, in addition to a restless nature, reveals minor nervous disorders. A blue spot on the life line can, at an advanced age, indicate circulatory disorders. A black spot is often seen after heavy drinking, but need not cause concern.

A thick heart line

'On close examination of my palm I find that I have quite a thick heart line and, contrastingly, a wavy life line. What does this mean?'

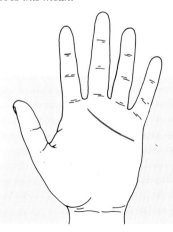

It means that you have a passionate, overbearing nature. You pour out your feelings in a torrent when the circumstances so justify. The features that you mention are generally combined with a very long first phalange of the thumb. An over-emotional nature is often associated with deliberately short nails. It is not unusual for nervous disorders to arise, but the will to live and to love is, without a shadow of a doubt, predominant.

Head and life lines are joined

'I should like to know whether the head line indicates a person's intelligence only, or also mental health. My head line, at the start, is joined to the life line for almost two centimetres. What does this mean?'

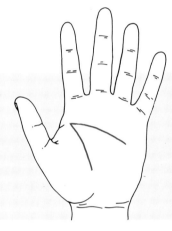

The head line is connected to everything associated with mental activity – intelligence, intellectual capabilities, the way of thinking and, at the same time, the state of the cerebral and nervous systems.

The fact that the head line is joined to the life line for a certain distance indicates a slightly shy and insecure person who, from fear of making a mistake, depends a great deal on others and is influenced by current opinions. This characteristic is not only negative – it also has a positive aspect. Such a person has an ability to listen to others, and to put himself or herself in the other person's place.

How can you tell if two people are compatible?

'I have a very deep heart line, while the person I love has a very thin one. Is there a risk that we shall be unable to reach any understanding in matters of the heart?'

From a careful examination of the heart line it is possible to determine not only the degree of generosity and human warmth but also a person's ability to give himself or herself over entirely to love. A very deep heart line denotes a passionate temperament, while a very thin one is characteristic of individuals who tend to be self-contained and introverted. In general, these people limit their affections to the family circle, reducing their friendships to the minimum. In this case the two people have different ways of expressing love but this does not mean that it is not possible for them to reach an understanding. Given the law of opposites, the attraction is very strong and each can become complementary to the other. Remember, too, that the lines of the hand are not fixed, and the heart line can change considerably over the years in the most unexpected manner.

Discoloured fingernails

'Exactly a year ago I suffered a heavy blow to the thumbnail of the right hand, which turned black in a somewhat ugly fashion. The problem has now resolved itself, but the nail still has a discoloured area that is causing me some concern. Is it true that the fingernails are indicators of our health?'

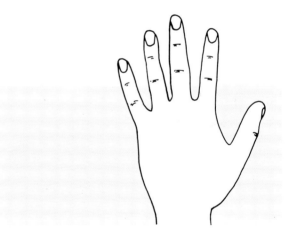

You are quite right in thinking that to an expert the fingernails can provide valuable information on the general state of health and in some cases they can be used as a means of identifying specific illnesses. In your case, however, what has happened is entirely normal. The discoloration that you see on your thumbnail is the equivalent of a scar that will only disappear in time. It is also possible that the mark will be permanent. Whether it disappears or remains it is totally innocuous and in no way indicative of ill health.

Many musicians do have delicate hands and fingers and it is often remarked if a child develops long, slender hands that he or she may be a potential pianist. The assumption is that you need long fingers in order to span the width of the keys, whereas you really need almost flexible ones. Although many people still adhere to the former belief, there are almost as many exceptions to the rule: Vivaldi's and Toscanini's hands were anything but beautiful. Among pianists, neither Maurizio Pollini has, nor Duke Ellington (pictured here) had, particularly slender fingers. A good performer of music must first and foremost have considerable agility in his or her fingers, as well as extremely quick reflexes. Quite long, pointed fingers indicate an artistic, or sometimes philosophical, bent, but do not necessarily belong to a musician – your hands are just as much those of a musician.

When the fate line is missing

'After looking carefully at my hand I have succeeded in finding the fate line. However, one of my acquaintances does not have one at all. Does this mean that I have a predetermined fate and she doesn't?'

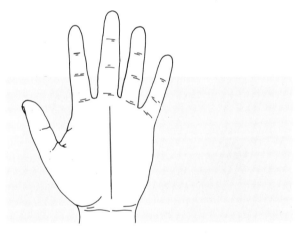

The fate line, which is also known as the line of Saturn or the line of fortune, starts at the wrist, crosses the head and heart lines and extends to the base of the middle finger. This line is found in its entirety in only 11 cases out of 100. In another 38 cases out of 100 it does not extend beyond the head line: there are 37 cases in 100 in which it does not reach as far as the heart line. In 14 cases it is missing entirely, as on your acquaintance's hand.

The absence of this line does not mean the absence of a predetermined or happy fate. It means only that success will have to be gained on the person's own merits, without relying on strokes of luck.

Duke Ellington, the American jazz composer, pianist and conductor

The Pianist's Hand

'Is it true that people who play the piano well have slender, pale hands? I adore music and seem to be very good at it, but far from having slim hands, I have rather large ones and my fingers are quite stubby.'

The relationship between hand and profession

'I have been told that some jobs actually require particular hands. I can understand how this might be possible, but I should like some further explanations.'

Christian Barnard performed the first human heart transplant

There is no doubt that most jobs are better done when performed by those who have suitable hands for the purpose. Everyone knows that a pianist needs agile hands and fingers that are capable of moving at high speed. No-one would doubt that a good watchmaker needs a light touch and perfectly controlled fingers. It is less commonly realized that no surgeon could excel in his profession unless he had hands and fingers of steel.

Migraines

'I know that there is a form of palmistry known as medical chiromancy that is able, by reading the hand, to establish a predisposition or otherwise to certain illnesses. I should like to know something about cephalalgia, (headache), a disorder that afflicts many people and that, while not serious, becomes distressing when chronic.'

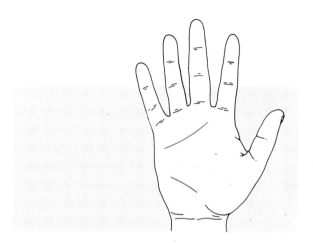

This is quite true. Cephalalgia, or a headache, can reach levels of pain and persistence that are truly intolerable. To establish the tendency to suffer from this type of illness, it is necessary to examine the head line carefully. If it is twisted in chains along its entire path, has short breaks, or is sloping or intersected by a number of bars, this means that the person's psyche is easily tired or that he or she becomes upset by emotional stresses that encourage migraine. A red and irregular line of Mercury can also indicate a certain predisposition to poor functioning of the liver and consequently to the symptom of migraine. The gravity of all these signs is diminished if the hand overall denotes vitality and good physical and mental health.

A limp handshake

'I have noticed that some people, on shaking hands, do not exert any pressure. The impression that I get from them is one of uneasiness; I don't know why but I always think that anyone who offers a limp hand is insincere. Am I wrong, or is there some foundation to my belief?'

This question relates to the field of general psychology rather than to a study of the hand. The sensation that we get on shaking a limp hand is indeed one of uneasiness, almost as if the person in question were refusing to establish an open relationship. In general, this type of attitude is inherent in people who are relatively inactive and do not like contact with others. Everyone is familiar with what is defined as a 'sportsman's handshake' – an energetic and possibly too hard handshake – which is a sign of exhibitionism. The limp hand also conflicts with the rules of etiquette. There is a precise reason for the development of the handshake: it is a demonstration of trust in the other person which was originally designed to show there was no concealed weapon in the hand.

Index

Acknowledgments

Editor: Carolyn Pyrah
Copy Editor: Diana Vowles
Art Editor: Brazzle Atkins
Design: Design 23
Artwork: Brazzle Atkins
Picture Research: Rachel Duffield
Production Controller: Garry Lewis

The publishers would like to thank the following for their
kind permission to reproduce the photographs
in this book:

Don Caroll/Image Bank 74; Geoffrey Gove/Image Bank 19;
Steven Hunt/Image Bank 6, 54; Janeart Ltd/Image Bank 66;
Don Landwehrle/Image Bank 42; Sandra Lousada/Susan
Griggs 65; Michael Tcherekoff/Image Bank 32; Chris Alan
Wilton/Image Bank 10; Zefa 61.